MEMENTO MORI

Also by Peter Jones

Vote for Caesar

Learn Latin: The Book of the
Daily Telegraph *QED Series*

Veni, Vidi, Vici

Eureka!

Quid Pro Quo

MEMENTO MORI

WHAT THE ROMANS CAN TELL US ABOUT OLD AGE & DEATH

PETER JONES

Atlantic Books
London

First published in hardback in Great Britain in 2018 by Atlantic Books,
an imprint of Atlantic Books Ltd.

1 2 3 4 5 6 7 8 9

A CIP catalogue record for this book is available from the British Library.

Hardback ISBN: 978-1-78649-480-1
E-book ISBN: 978-1-78649-481-8
Paperback ISBN: 978-1-78649-482-5

Printed in Great Britain

CONTENTS

ACKNOWLEDGEMENTS

The copious sources for this topic of suitably undying interest reside in the Bibliography. Tim G. Parkin's *Old Age in the Roman World* remained the key point of reference. I am extremely grateful to Colin Leach and Jeannie Cohen for help with a number of problems.

The little poem by Ausonius and comment by Marcus Aurelius (see pp. 191–2) sum up my feelings on the subject.

Peter Jones
Newcastle upon Tyne
April 2018

INTRODUCTION

All modern books announce that, thanks to advances in diet and medicine, old age is an exciting new phenomenon with endless possibilities. Soon we shall all be able to make it our ambition to live for ever or die in the attempt. Adam would rather sniff at that – he lived to 930 – and so would Methuselah, who holds the biblical world record at 969. These are, however, positive teenagers compared with the Sumerian kings of ancient Babylon (modern Iraq), of whom En-men-lu-anna clocked in at 43,200.

The wrath of God at least sorted out the biblical heroes. Abraham only made it to 175, Isaac to 180 and Joseph to 110, and at Genesis 6:3 God fixed the span of human life at a generous 120 years. Recent studies in Canada suggest that 125 should be reachable. So when you reached sixty, you would have another whole wonderful lifetime to go, adding all the burdens of the first 60 years to the next 60. What a prospect. But then prediction is always difficult, especially when it refers to the future.

Ancient Greeks and the Psalms, more realistically, came up with around three score years and ten. They, however, should have been so lucky. In the battle against Hannibal at Cannae (216 BC) the Romans lost some 50,000 men in one day. In AD 165 Marcus

Cornelius Fronto wrote to his close friend the emperor Marcus Aurelius:

> I have lost five children in the most wretched circumstances of my life, all five separately, each an only child, and suffering this series of bereavements in such a way that no child was born to me except when I was already bereaved. So I always lost children without any left to comfort me, and procreated others with my grief still fresh upon me.

From AD 165 to 180, a plague, starting in the East and returning nine years later, killed probably about 5 million people. Three score years and ten were quite a few years too many for most of the population.

So it is not surprising that, as far back as records allow us to go, old age was often seen as something precious and probably the work of the gods, and the old were therefore rich sources of experience and wisdom (an African motto states 'When an old man dies, a library burns down'). Not, as we shall see, that Aristotle would agree. Further, in the classical world we regularly find that old age was rather to be feared, because of increasing physical and mental decline.

Contrast today. We can hardly move for oldies and – thanks to birth control, female education and declining poverty – *globally* we are now almost at 'peak' babies. So it is going to get worse: population will grow only because oldies refuse to help out by signing a 'do not resuscitate' form. And that raises the question 'To what purpose?' Life for its own sake? It looks like it, given the enthusiasm with which medical services spend their resources on keeping us oldies alive at all costs (about *half* the NHS budget is spent on the over-65s) merely guaranteeing that all the sooner will they run out of money to spend on the young. No wonder age is not held in honour. No wonder ageing journalists try to buck us all up by announcing that eighty is the 'new twenty' (though as Tom Stoppard pointed out, it is actually the new ninety). Naturally, there is nothing wrong with hankering after the philosopher Plato's ideal:

> In the eyes of the majority, the highest condition attainable by a human being is to be rich, healthy and honoured, live to an old age and, after burying one's parents decently, to be decently buried by one's own children, in magnificent style.

But it was an ideal because virtually no one actually realized it. Today the price of realizing it seems to be pedalling the highways or pounding the pavements in Day-Glo lycra, breath reeking of Horlicks: the (old) boot-camp theory of ageing. Nobody remembers the ancient Greek adage 'Call no man happy until he is dead' – on the grounds that life could throw any number of spanners into the ointment before the curtain fell, and the later it fell, the more intense the hail of spanners. That said, a newspaper announced as I write that life is shortened by drinking more than a bottle of wine a week. What splendid news for all!

This book contains a rich melange of ancient sources about old age and death. It concentrates on the Romans, but they (as they acknowledged) were in heavy cultural debt to the Greeks; so Homer, Plato, the physician Hippocrates and Aristotle have walk-on parts too. Seneca, the Roman philosopher and millionaire adviser to Emperor Nero, wrote copiously and at length on these topics, while the statesman and thinker Cicero, the keen letter-writer and senator Pliny the Younger, the Greek essayist Plutarch (writing in Roman times) and a huge range of Latin epitaphs will also feature large.

It will rapidly become clear that, thanks to the ancients, with their usual unwavering eye fixed firmly on the world as it is, all the problems associated with old age and death that so transfix us today were dealt with two millennia ago. But that only raises the question: is the modern world capable of facing the world as it is? *Memento mori* means 'remember you die'.

NOTES

One recent calculation concluded that 55 per cent of the Roman population lived at subsistence level, a maximum of 19 per cent just above it, and 10–22 per cent below it. Perhaps 5–10 per cent were in a relatively comfortable 'middling' group. That left the fabulously wealthy, highly educated elite at about 0.5 per cent of the population. It is their voices that dominate our sources, and so our perception of the Roman world. And those voices were effectively all male.

According to one statistic, one third of UK families live in poverty. On the grounds that in the ancient world subsistence was about the best one could hope for (and still is in parts of the modern world), a Roman might have said that far fewer Romans did (only 10–22 per cent).*

'Freedmen' refers to slaves that had been freed, and therefore became Roman citizens, a remarkably common occurrence in Rome. They maintained close connections with their 'patron', i.e. the owner who freed them.

---

* It ought to be pointed out that living in poverty in the United Kingdom is defined as living on less than 60 per cent of the median wage. Since it is likely that there will always be some people living at that level, there will nearly always be people automatically defined as 'poor'. But I add that, mathematically, it is possible for that not to be the case.

Chapter One

LIFESPAN

HOW LONG DID ROMANS LIVE?

The 'ancient world' in this book will cover the period from *c.* 700 BC, when the West's first literature appeared in Greece, to the collapse of the Roman Empire in the West, i.e. roughly AD 500. During that time we have examples of people living to over 100. That is entirely possible. What is much more difficult to decide is the normal life expectation across the whole population.

Below are given the UK statistics for 2015. Those are the sorts of figures we would love to have for the ancient world. But though Romans *did* take censuses of male citizens and their property every five years, they appear only patchily in our sources.

Then again, about 100,000 tomb inscriptions (epitaphs) survive. These are extremely interesting for all sorts of reasons, recording everyone from consuls to slaves to professional buffoons. But they are unreliable for census purposes, because they are too selective, being dominated by adult males. The same is true of written records – as will become clear.

UK STATISTICS

Our 'census' is taken over from Latin *census*, 'registration'. In Rome, this information was used to classify male citizens for class, military and tax purposes.

In the United Kingdom the Office for National Statistics produces an annual *population* count. In 2015, out of a population of 65.1 million:

- 1.5 million were above 85 (2.3 per cent)
- 11.6 million were over 65 (17.8 per cent)
- 23.6 million were over 50 (36.2 per cent)
- There are now more people in the UK over 65 than there are under 18
- Half a million were over 90 (70 per cent of them women)
- The life expectancy at birth for females is 82.8, and for males 79.1
- A girl born in 2011 has a 1 in 3 chance, a boy a 1 in 4 chance, of living to 100
- The median age is now 40, the highest it has ever been 'Median age' is not the average age: it means the age at which half the population is younger, half older.

The latest figures for 2016 show a small increase on all these figures: for example, total population 65.6 million, over-85s 2.4 per cent, and so on.

ROMAN TOMBSTONES:
AN IMPOSSIBLE PICTURE

The Roman Empire at its height numbered perhaps 60 million; the total of lives over the *c.* 500 years during which the Empire survived, far more. From this period we have recovered *c.* 100,000 funerary inscriptions from across the Roman world. This looks like vital evidence for demographic purposes, i.e. describing the size, structure and distribution of the population. But for that purpose it is, in fact, largely useless.

DODGY STATS

There are 10,697 epitaphs from Roman North Africa. These yield the following statistics:

26.5 per cent (2,835) lived to 70 or over;

2.96 per cent (313) to 100 or over; and

0.25 per cent (27) to 120 or over.

Now look at the UK statistics. It seems unlikely that (given diet, disease, medical understanding, etc.) Roman North Africa's ancient population could have so easily outlived today's UK population.

DODGIER STATS

In one region of North Africa tombstone data from 1,258 individuals would suggest that:

The average life expectancy was 60.2;

39.3 per cent (494 people) were over 70; but only

0.5 per cent (6) were under 10!

This is obviously absurd and confirms the point about the unreliability of epitaphs as evidence for age statistics. The fact is that tombstones marked the death of someone precious. So they could not add up to a serious record of a whole society's age range or life expectancy. If they told one anything, it would be about why the deceased was important to the family or friends who paid for the monument to be put up.

Finally, when one *does* collate the information from all of them and try to draw demographic conclusions, the result describes a society the like of which has never existed anywhere at any time: a high preponderance of males over females, and very few babies (calculations vary from 0.4 per cent to 1.3 per cent!).

WRITTEN RECORDS

Pliny the Elder's 37-volume encyclopedia (*Natural History*) of the Roman world survives complete. One section was devoted to human longevity. Apart from the obviously mythical or transparently dodgy, he mentioned a few over-100s: a man who lived to 108, and a woman to 115 (she also bore 15 children). The actress Galeria Copiola appeared on stage aged 104 to celebrate Augustus' recovery from illness in AD 8. Nothing wrong with that: it is entirely feasible that very rare individuals did live to such an advanced age.

DODGIER WRITTEN RECORDS

Pliny quoted a census from AD 74. One might expect serious information from such a source. But using the census from *one* region of Italy, Pliny reported that:

81 people survived into their 100s, including

4 up to 135 or 137; and

3 up to 140.

This strains credulity somewhat. The reason may possibly be that all the people quoted were born before Augustus introduced a system of birth registration, set up in AD 4 and AD 9. How, therefore, the census could have been certain of their birth dates is not clear.

ROMAN LIFE EXPECTANCY

Epitaphs and written records do not give us any demographic help. What, then, can we do? Make a best guess is the answer, with the help of reliable life statistics from the nineteenth and twentieth centuries. These life statistics, gathered from very different cultures all over the world, are used by insurance companies to work out the likelihood of *this* sort of person with *this* sort of lifestyle at *this* age (etc.) living for – how much longer? Scholars proceed as follows:

First, the birth and death rate of any ancient population we know about must have been of such a sort as to create a stable society. That means enough children survived for long enough to have children themselves. If that was not the case, the society would have died out.

Second, scholars make a guess at the *average* age expectancy of the population: in this case, our guess is about twenty-five years. Why? Because lower than twenty and the society would have died out; but to get it above thirty, the ancients would need to have had a far better understanding of illness, hygiene, diet (etc.) than they did (see p. 66). Further, the evidence from the written record as a whole – including, for example, tax records, legal texts, censuses and so on

– does not make it wildly unlikely that an average life expectancy of about twenty-five years is wrong.

So, making those assumptions, scholars ask the question: what would be the life expectancy of a stable society whose average age was twenty-five?

WORLD RECORDS

Coale-Demeny life tables were constructed in 1966 by the Americans Ansley Coale and Paul Demeny. They were derived from 192 life tables based on a range of statistical records, some before 1900, some after the Second World War. Of those tables, 176 came from Europe, America, Australia and New Zealand and a sprinkling of the rest from Africa, Asia, Japan, etc.

On the strength of those records, it is assumed that in the ancient world – bar peaks and troughs for special circumstances – conclusions can be drawn about the lifespans of a stable population whose age expectancy was twenty-five. Of course, while the percentages given accurately reflect the statistics, they are far too precise to reflect the reality of the very different regions of the ancient world.

LESS DODGY STATS

Current best guesses about the ancient world derived from life tables suggest:

About a third of babies died within a month or so of birth; about half would be dead by the age of 5. Disease, bad diet and poor hygiene would be the main killers.

c. 50 per cent of the population was 20 or under.

Nearly 80 per cent was dead by 50.

What a nightmare – a world dominated by teenagers! Contrast nowadays, where over 20 per cent of the population is 65 and over – actually *more* than the number under 18.

HOW MANY MORE YEARS TO LIVE?

Imagine a cohort of 100,000 Roman babies born at the same time.

At age 1 – 65,000 would be alive; at age 5 – 50,000; at age 10 – 48,000; at age 20 – 43,500; at age 30 – 36,500; at age 40 – 30,000; at age 50 – 21,000; at age 60 – 13,000; at 70 – 5,500.

AN INFORMED ANCIENT GUESS

A Roman lawyer called Ulpian (c. AD 170–223) produced a practical life table of his own. Its purpose is not clear: it has been suggested that it was used to calculate the value of maintenance bequests left in wills. It is clearly unscientific, but the results look roughly along the right lines:

Current age	Further years expected
Up to 19	30
20–24	28
25–29	25
30–34	22
35–39	20
40–49	19, reducing by 1 year annually to 10
50–54	9
55–59	7
60 and over	5

WOMEN TAKE THE STRAIN

A high death rate is usually matched by high fertility, and it needed to be if the Roman population was to remain stable. Given widowhood, sterility, divorce and so on, every woman would have had to give birth to between 6 and 9 children to keep up replacement levels. Here are three grim examples of family loss:

The epitaph of one Veturia recorded that she died aged 27 after 16 years of marriage, having lost 5 of her 6 children.

The political reformers Tiberius and Gaius Gracchus and their sister Sempronia (second century BC) were the only three siblings to survive out of nine.

The emperor Marcus Aurelius and his wife Faustina had 13 children. Marcus died in AD 180. Only 5 of his children survived him.

DEMOGRAPHICS AND THE *PATERFAMILIAS*

A feature of Roman life that Romans saw as unique to themselves was the position of the *paterfamilias*, early Latin for the 'father' (*pater*) of the 'household' (*familia*). This was the belief that the *paterfamilias* had complete authority over everyone and everything in his household. He was the master of family, persons and property, to such an extent that one could own nothing over which the *paterfamilias* did not have total control right up until the moment of his death. This could raise the faintly absurd prospect of a *paterfamilias* living to, say, 85 (like Cato the Elder) and continuing to rule over sons and grandsons who were consuls! But as the age statistics suggest, *c.* 70 per cent of sons would be fatherless by the age of 25, and 95 per cent would be by the age of 40. So if there was a problem with Papa, it would not last long. One consequence would be many underage children living with relatives or under guardianship.

THE LIVING FAMILY

Latin had names for grandfather/mother going up to great-great-great-great-grandfather/mother. But *living* grandparents rarely featured in the literature. The reason is that (as the full tables show) by the age of ten a Roman had only a 50-50 chance of having any grandparents alive; a Roman aged twenty would have less than a 1 in 100 chance of having their paternal grandfather still alive, women being slightly more long-lived.

So, although grandparents from the mother's side would be more common, grandparents generally were not a big presence in Roman children's lives. An exception was the mother of Quintilian, whose young wife died at 19, leaving granny with the main job of raising their two sons – both of whom died young (see p. 51).

GLADIATORS

Some occupations were more dangerous than others. Gladiatorial combat is an obvious example. A large number of inscriptions recorded gladiatorial deaths, and among them we find, for example, from a gladiatorial training school in Venusia (southern Italy), the names of at least 29 dead gladiators:

- 10 were trainees, who died before they ever entered the ring (presumably from training accidents or illness)

- 19 died during or after fighting – 3 after 1 fight; 4 after 2; 3 after 3; 1 after 4; 2 after 5; 1 after 6; 2 after 7; and 3 after 12.

Other inscriptions gave ages. We find a gladiator

- aged 23, dying after 8 fights
- aged 27, dying after 11 fights
- aged 34, dying after 21 fights
- aged 30, dying after 34 fights (won 21, drawn 9, lost 4).

Surviving inscriptions from Pompeii recorded that a quarter of the gladiators had more than ten years' experience, and the remainder less. Meanwhile, in a gladiatorial graveyard from Ephesus in Roman-occupied Asia Minor (Turkey), 68 bodies have been identified, all but 2 being males aged between 20 and 30.

Put together, all the available gladiatorial statistics suggest a *median* lifespan of 22.5.

As to the purpose of these games, Romans loved to see blood spilled, but equally they wanted a good fight. So a popular fighter who surrendered would probably be allowed to live, so that he could fight again – we hear of some winning between 60 and 150 fights – as would any man who put on a good show (see p. 86).

ANCIENT VIEWS OF AGE STAGES

The statistics on p.12 offer us the best guess we can make at the prospects of life for a newborn child. For those that survived, the Roman envisaged a number of possible life stages. Generally, they thought of three: youth, maturity and old age. The Greek philosopher

Pythagoras (*c.* 580–*c.* 500 BC) was the first classical 'four-arc' man. For him these consisted of twenty-year stages: 0–20 childhood, 20–40 adolescence, 40–60 youth and 60–80 old age. Still young at 59, eh? Pythagoras clearly anticipated all those panting 'life-stylists' with their fast-flowing biros who now proclaim 59 to be the new 16.

The four arcs of life

The scabrously witty and often lyrical poet Martial wrote a poem celebrating his birthday. It was 1 March and he was 57 (the late AD 90s). Far from putting on a party and being given presents, in our fashion, the Roman birthday boy carried out a religious ritual on his *own* behalf, celebrating *himself* and praying for many more such happy anniversaries. So Martial duly offered the usual cakes and smoking incense to the gods and now asked for eighteen more years, to bring him up to 75, when he would have completed 'the three arcs of life'. The fourth was piteous senility, on which he was not so keen. The gods did not grant his wish: he died in his sixties.

The medical four

Why did Pythagoras choose four 'arcs' of life? One answer is because it connected with medical theory.

Ancient doctors believed that bodily health was controlled by the balance of four liquids ('humours') in the body: blood, phlegm, yellow bile and black bile. These could be related to other natural phenomena in fours: earth, air, fire and water (the four basic constituents of the world); heat, cold, wetness and dryness; and most importantly for Pythagoras (perhaps), the four seasons: spring, summer, autumn and winter. As one doctor explained, the *child* was wet and warm (like spring), the *youth* dry and warm (summer), the *man* dry and cold (autumn), and the *old man* wet and cold (winter). Indeed, such was the influence of the four humours of ancient thought down the millennia that even the four Gospels were made to fit the sequence!

Solon's ten stages

Solon (*c.* 640–*c.* 560 BC), an important political reformer (and poet) in Athens, produced the first Greek account of man's ages – ten of them in all – in seven-year units.

The ten ages can be summarized as follows. Note that Solon was here thinking of the physical and political/social development of an aristocratic male, dedicated to serving his society to the best of his ability. Women need not apply.

1–7:	grows and loses first teeth
8–14:	first signs of physical maturity slowly appear
15–21:	still growing, fuzzy chin, skin changing colour
22–28:	peak of strength, 'when men show they are men'
29–35:	time to marry and produce sons to continue the line
36–42:	altogether sensible, no more irresponsible behaviour
43–49 } 50–56 }	wisdom and eloquence at their peak
57–63:	capable, but losing a degree of mental grip
64–70:	time to hand in the dinner-pail.

The seven-year stages are probably a result of Greek beliefs about the 'magic' of certain numbers. Seven and its multiples (especially multiples of the equally 'magical' three) had a long history of significance in ancient thought, for good or ill: seven planets, days of the week (based on the Old Testament account of the genesis of the world), seven Arabic holy temples, ancient Buddhas, Hindu chakras, Deadly Sins, notes in the scale, colours in the rainbow and so on.

The seven-stage theory

Hippocrates (469–399 BC), the famous Greek physician, favoured a 7 x 7 analysis, as an ancient dictionary item tells us:

> There are seven ages, according to Hippocrates:
>
> | | |
> |---|---|
> | from 1 to 7 | (called a 'young child') |
> | from 7 to 14 | ('boy') |
> | from 14 to 21 | ('adolescent') |
> | from 21 to 28 | ('young man') |
> | from 28 to 35 | ('man') |
> | from 35 to 42 | ('elder') |
> | from 42 to 49 | ('old man'). |

Oh dear! An old man at 42! But this, at least, acknowledges the hard fact of the lessening chance of living beyond 50.

Dangerous years

On his sixty-fourth birthday the emperor Augustus wrote to his grandson Gaius, beginning: 'Hullo, Gaius, my dearest little donkey.' He said he hoped that Gaius, too, had celebrated

in health and happiness my sixty-fourth year, since I have now
passed the most dangerous point of my life, common to all older
men – the sixty-third year.

Do the sums: 63 is 7 x 3 x 3. No wonder the writer quoting this
letter added: 'For almost all old men, the most dangerous age is 63,
characterized by some danger and disaster involving serious illness,
or loss of life or dementia.' The ages of 49 (7 x 7) and 81 (9 x 9) were
equally suspect.

Clarity, please!

Romans also had a five-stage sequence, but by this time one is
beginning to lose one's grip on reality. That feeling is confirmed by
the observation that, depending on which ancient system you believed
in, 'old age' could begin at any of the following ages: 42, 46, 48, 49,
56, 60, 63, 69, 70 and 77!

'Youth' was equally flexible. Surviving epitaphs apply the term
'young man' to individuals who had died at the ages of 16 and 50, in
these two cases describing both as 'in the flower of their youth'. Some
flower.

The fact is that these exact divisions were not the result of any close
observation of human physical or social reality, but of superstitious
beliefs based on number magic (as we have seen) and astrology, with
help from philosophers trying to impose their own patterns on a
messy world.

Chapter Two

YOUNG VERSUS OLD
A BRIEF DIGRESSION

YOUNG AND OLD: A ROMAN VIEW

The Roman poet Horace came up with a four-part theory of life, based on the characteristics which the audience at the theatre would *expect* to find in the depiction of any age group. This view tended to emphasize those aspects of age that lent themselves to stereotyping and made for good dramatic conflict:

the child, who liked to play with friends, fly equally quickly into – and out of – a temper, and changed from minute to minute;

the young man, free at last from school, who liked active sports, did not like being told what to do, had strong passions and no interest in practicalities;

adults, consumed with ambition, seeking wealth and friends; and *the old*, who turned miserly, put things off, feared for the future, objected to the young and generally looked back fondly on what they did in their youth.

While such sentiments about the old were regularly rehearsed in ancient literature, there was another side too.

HOMER'S VIEW

Whatever physical degradation old age inflicted (see p. 63), the epic poet Homer respected the old for their wisdom, even if it brought a good deal of garrulity with it. The old man Nestor was the prime example of such wisdom in Homer. His garrulity was justified because wisdom was based on experience, and that experience needed explaining to the young.

In Homer's *Iliad*, when the Greeks at Troy debated how to bring Achilles back into the fighting, the youthful Diomedes said they did not need him. Nestor replied that he admired Diomedes, but:

> You are a young man – there's no denying it – and in fact you could be my youngest son. Your words are intelligent and what you have said is wholly appropriate. But I am much older than you are, and it is now time for me to speak out and take the whole situation into consideration.

That was the positive take on old age. Aristotle was not so sure, and such was his authority that many Romans were not so sure either.

EXPECTATIONS OF THE CHILD

Homeric children were often highlighted for the future hopes invested in them. Hector, the Trojan hero of Homer's *Iliad*, prayed that his son Astyanax might become a better soldier than his father. Achilles' old tutor Phoenix said that his job had been to make Achilles 'a speaker . . . and a man of action', but he also confessed that, being childless himself,

> I tried to make you my son, godlike Achilles, so that some day you would save me from an unhappy old age.

Here, then, were themes picked up by the Romans: the child must be taught how to become a great war-leader (just like his father), which would require not only military skills – obviously – but also the capacity to win arguments in debate about policy. Then again, children owed their parents – and those who raised them – a duty of reciprocal care as the years went by (pp. 69–70). That Achilles himself, doomed to die young, would never return home to protect his father Peleus was a constant refrain in the *Iliad*.

HOT STUFF

Aristotle took the view that internal 'heat' was the key to life, and the loss of it resulted in death. So preservation of heat was vital for life, and that was the function of the body's cooling mechanisms: they helped to conserve that vital heat. Aristotle used the analogy of banking up a fire to keep it going.

'Heat', therefore was characteristic of the vigorous young, whose cooling mechanisms helped them preserve it. But it did not take much to tip the old and cold, whose mechanisms as a whole started to seize up, from life to death: as Sophocles made one of his characters say: 'a small tilt of the balance puts ancient bodies to sleep'.

For Aristotle, then, heat and cold explained the differences between young and old, which he developed as follows.

ARISTOTLE ON THE YOUNG

In his work on rhetoric, Aristotle came up with suggestions for the sort of persuasive assertions which an advocate could work with in developing a case relating to the young and old. Here is Aristotle's analysis of, firstly, the young, then the old, and finally those in their prime of life. The numbers in square brackets in the section on the young are picked up in the opposite sense in the section on the old:

YOUTHFUL PASSIONS

Young men have strong passions, and tend to gratify them indiscriminately.

Of the bodily desires, it is the sexual by which they are most swayed and in which they show [1] absence of self-control. They are changeable and fickle in their desires, which are violent while they last, but quickly over: [2] their impulses are keen but not deep-rooted, and are like sick people's attacks of hunger and thirst.

They are hot-tempered and quick-tempered, and apt to give way to their anger; bad temper often gets the better of them, for owing to their love of honour they cannot bear to be slighted, and are indignant if they imagine themselves unfairly treated.

While they love honour, they love victory still more; for youth is eager for superiority over others, and victory is one form of this.

[3] They love both more than they love money, which indeed they love very little, not having yet learned what it means to be without it.

They look at the good side rather than the bad, [4] not having yet witnessed many instances of wickedness.

They are sanguine; nature warms their blood as though with excess of wine; and besides that, [4] they have as yet met with few disappointments. [5] They trust others readily, because they have not yet often been cheated. Because of this, they are easily cheated.

[6] Their lives are mainly spent not in memory but in expectation; for expectation refers to the future, memory to the past, and youth has a long future before it and a short past behind it: on the first day of one's life one has nothing at all to remember, and can only look forward.

[7] Their hot tempers and hopeful dispositions make them more courageous than older men are; the hot temper prevents fear, and [8] the hopeful disposition creates confidence; we cannot feel fear so long as we are feeling angry, and any expectation of good makes us confident.

YOUTHFUL IDEALISM

They are shy, accepting the rules of society in which they have been trained, and not yet believing in any other standard of honour.

[9] They have exalted notions, because they have not yet been humbled by life or learned its necessary limitations; moreover, their hopeful disposition makes them think themselves equal to great things – and that means having exalted notions.

[9] They would always rather do noble deeds than useful ones: their lives are regulated more by moral feeling than by reasoning; and [10] whereas reasoning leads us to choose what is useful, moral goodness leads us to choose what is noble.

They are fonder of their friends, intimates and companions than older men are, because they like spending their days in the company of others, and have not yet come to value either their friends or anything else by their usefulness to themselves.

YOUTHFUL EXCESS

All their mistakes are in the direction of doing things excessively and vehemently. They [11] overdo everything, they love too much and hate too much, and the same thing with everything else.

[12] They think they know everything, and are always quite sure about it; this, in fact, is why [11] they overdo everything. [13] If they do wrong to others, it is because they mean to insult them, not to do them actual harm.

[14] They are ready to pity others, because they think everyone an honest man, or anyhow better than he is: they judge their neighbour by their own harmless natures, and so cannot think he deserves to be treated in that way.

[15] They are fond of fun and therefore witty, wit being well-bred insolence.

Such, then, is the character of the young.

ARISTOTLE ON THE OLD

Men who are past their prime may be said to be formed for the most part of elements that are the contrary of all these.

They have lived many years; [4] they have often been taken in, and often made mistakes; and life on the whole is a bad business. [11] The result is that they are sure about nothing and underdo everything. [12] They 'think', but they never 'know'; and because of their hesitation they always add a 'possibly' or a 'perhaps', putting everything this way, and nothing positively.

ELDERLY SMALL-MINDEDNESS

[5] They are cynical; that is, they tend to put the worse construction on everything. Further, their experience makes them [8] distrustful and therefore suspicious of evil. Consequently [11] they neither love warmly nor hate bitterly, but they love as though they will some day hate, and hate as though they will some day love.

[9] They are small-minded, because they have been humbled by life: their desires are set upon nothing more exalted or unusual than what will help them to keep alive. They are too fond of themselves; this is one form that small-mindedness takes. Because of this, they guide their lives too much by considerations of [9] what is useful and too little by what is noble – for the useful is what is good for oneself, and [10] the noble what is good absolutely. They are not shy, but shameless rather; caring less for what is noble than for what is useful, they feel contempt for what people may think of them.

[3] They are not generous, because money is one of the things

they must have, and at the same time their experience has taught them how hard it is to get and how easy to lose.

[7] They are cowardly, and are always anticipating danger; unlike that of the young, who are warm-blooded, their temperament is chilly; old age has paved the way for cowardice; fear is, in fact, a form of chill. [8] They lack confidence in the future; partly through experience – for [4] most things go wrong, or anyhow turn out worse than one expects; and partly because of their cowardice.

They love life; and all the more [6] when their last day has come (man desires what is absent), and also because we desire most strongly that which we need most urgently.

ELDERLY JOYLESSNESS

[6] They live by memory rather than by hope; for what is left to them of life is but little as compared with the long past; and hope refers to the future, memory to the past. This, again, is the cause of their loquacity; they are continually talking of the past, because they enjoy remembering it.

[2] Their fits of anger are sudden but feeble. Their sensual passions have either gone completely or have lost their vigour: consequently they do not feel their passions much, and their actions are inspired less by what they feel than by [3] love of gain. [1] Hence men at this time of life are often supposed to have a self-controlled character; the fact is that their passions have slackened, and they are slaves to the love of gain.

[10] They guide their lives by reasoning more than by moral feeling; reasoning being directed to utility and moral feeling to moral goodness. [13] If they wrong others, they mean to injure them, not to insult them.

[14] Old men may feel pity, as well as young men, but not for the same reason. Young men feel it out of kindness; old men out of weakness, imagining that anything that befalls anyone else might easily happen to them, which, as we saw, is a thought that excites pity. [15] Hence they are querulous, and not disposed to jesting or laughter – the love of laughter being the very opposite of querulousness.

ARISTOTLE'S MIDDLE WAY

Aristotle's account of the old is rather depressing. The reason is that he believed that the 'middle way' in life was always preferable. Consequently, the young and old, being at extremes, could not by definition show life at its best. That blessed state was therefore reserved for those in the middle or at their prime, as Aristotle put it:

As for men in their prime, clearly we shall find that they have a character between that of the young and that of the old, free from the extremes of either:

- They have neither that excess of **confidence** which amounts to rashness, nor too much **timidity**, but the right amount of each.
- They neither **trust** everybody nor **distrust** everybody, but judge people correctly.
- Their lives will be guided not by the sole consideration either of what is **noble** or of what is **useful**, but by both;
- Neither by **parsimony** nor by **prodigality**, but by what is **fit** and **proper**.
- So, too, in regard to **anger** and **desire**.

- They will be **brave** as well as **temperate**, and **temperate** as well as **brave**.
- These virtues are divided between the young and the old; the young are **brave but intemperate**, the old **temperate but cowardly**.
- To put it generally, all the valuable qualities that youth and age divide between them are united in the prime of life, while all their excesses or defects are replaced by **moderation** and **fitness**.

This was typical of Aristotle's method of understanding the world about us: look for the opposites and then seek the 'mean', the middle way, the balance between the two. Consequently, wisdom, a very desirable quality, could not be a consequence of the greater experience of the old. And that may indeed be the case: after all, it depends how that experience is applied. As Seneca said, 'old age is full of pleasure if one knows how to use it . . . life is most enjoyable when we are going slowly downhill, before we hit the steep decline'. That's as may be, but since wisdom is the one potentially useful quality that the old could possibly claim for themselves, we oldies should cling on to it.

NO PLACE FOR THE OLD

As the man who invented biology, Aristotle was always asking the questions: 'Why does this animal behave as it does?' 'What is this bit of the body actually *for*?' 'Why is it in that location?' 'Why does it look like that?' and so on. In other words, he had a strong sense of *function*. That obviously raised the questions: 'What are the old for?' 'What function do they fulfil?' Aristotle, it seems, could find no answer. All he could say was that it was in the nature of man to die. Since he theorized that warmth and moisture kept men alive, then as the years passed they must become cold and dry. But why should they do that?

The main contributing factor, he argued, was reproduction. This drained the body of the nutrition it needed to stay alive. Plants died for the same reason, producing seed to reproduce themselves, though some (he agreed) could regrow parts, because they had 'the principle of life [*psukhê*, 'soul', cf. our psyche] in every part'. The modern evolutionary answer would also relate to reproduction, though for a quite different reason: by the time your sexual function was past it, you should (in theory at least) have passed on your genes to the next generation. You have therefore served your purpose, and consequently your body starts to decline.

RESPECT FOR AGE

Many disagreed with Aristotle. The call for youthful respect for the old was common in Roman literature:

CICERO (106–43 BC)

It is, then, the duty of a young man to show deference to his elders and to attach himself to the best and most approved of them, so as to receive the benefit of their counsel and influence. For the inexperience of youth requires the practical wisdom of age to strengthen and direct it ... The old, on the other hand, should, it seems, have their physical labours reduced; their mental activities should be actually increased. They should endeavour, too, by means of their counsel and practical wisdom to be of as much service as possible to their friends and to the young, and above all to the state.

AULUS GELLIUS (c. AD 130–c 180)

Among the earliest Romans, as a rule, neither birth nor wealth was more highly honoured than age, but older men were reverenced by their juniors almost like gods and like their own parents, and everywhere and in every kind of honour they were regarded as first and of prior right. From a dinner party, too, older men were escorted home by younger men, as we read in the records of the past, a custom which, as tradition has it, the Romans took over from the Spartans, by whom, in accordance with the laws of Lycurgus, greater honour on all occasions was paid to greater age.

THE AUGUSTAN HISTORY ON THE NEW EMPEROR TACITUS (c. AD 200–c. 276)

We have chosen as emperor a man advanced in years, one who will watch over all like a father. From him we need fear nothing ill-considered, nothing overhasty, nothing cruel. All his actions, we may predict, will be earnest, all dignified, and, in fact, what the republic herself would command ... Indeed, if you should wish to consider those monsters of old, a Nero, I mean, an Elagabalus, a Commodus – or rather, always, an 'Incommodious' – you would assuredly find that their vices were due as much to their youth as to the men themselves. May the gods forfend that we should give the title of emperor to a child or of Father of his Country to an immature boy.

THE YOUNG AND THEIR FUN

All very well: but whenever did the young obey their elders and betters? Cicero in a letter remembered how, when he was young, the old talked despairingly of the younger generation, and now here he was (aged 57) doing the same. But all Romans moaned about the youth of the day. At a time when they should be growing into adult responsibility, they were sex-mad, drank too much, gambled, got into street fights, ignored their education and spent all their time at the races, the amphitheatre (gladiators and wild animals) and the theatre (mimes – adventure stories with plenty of sex – and pantomime, single artistic performances).

Wealthy young men, we are told, would deck out their horses in fine trappings, gallop down busy streets where horses were not allowed, wear extravagant clothes (see-through togas!), perfume their curled and primped beards and hair, shave off their body hair and soften their skin like women, and so on – the opposite of virile, shaggy, bearded males, bulwarks of the battlefield and the Roman state.

For sex, there were slaves and brothels. The story was told of Cato the Elder congratulating a young man coming out of a brothel, on the grounds that it kept him away from young girls and married women. But when Cato kept on seeing him repeating the experience, he said he had not expected him to take up residence.

Nothing much new there, then. All part of the fun of 'growing up', what one used to call (after Shakespeare) one's 'salad days'. Daze, more like.

GENERATION GAP

There is probably no time when fathers and sons did not at some stage come into conflict, and no time when moralists did not debate the reasons for it, usually the pros and cons of too strict or too lax an upbringing. It was the same in Rome.

A comedy *The Brothers* by Terence (performed *c.* 160 BC) played on the family fortunes of two brothers, Micio and Demea. Demea had two sons, one of whom he gave to the unmarried Micio to raise. Micio loved his nephew dearly and gave him everything he wanted. Demea raised his other son rather severely. Here were Micio's reflections on his theory of upbringing:

> Demea is just too hard as a father, beyond rhyme or reason, and is quite wrong, in my view, to think that you gain strong, durable authority by force rather than affection. This is the theory I believe in. The boy who does what he has to simply because of the threat of punishment, will watch his back only if he thinks he will be found out. If not, he'll fall back on his natural inclinations. The one you win with kindness behaves sincerely, tries to do as he has been done by, and will be the same whether you are there or not. This is a father's duty, to get his son used to doing the right thing of his own free will rather than from fear of another. It's the difference between a father and a tyrant. The man who can't do that should admit he doesn't know how to manage children.

At the end, Demea had the last word:

> Micio, I wanted to show you that your reputation with your nephew for good nature and charm did not spring from an honest way

of life or what is fair and good, but from weakness, indulgence and extravagance. Now, boys, if you don't like my ways, because I don't humour you in absolutely everything, right or wrong, then forget it. Do whatever you like and spend like there's no tomorrow. On the other hand, you're young, short-sighted, headstrong and thoughtless, so you may prefer some advice or correction or help when needed. If so, here I am.

OLD GITS

Cicero said of old men on the Roman comic stage 'they are the stupidest of the characters, lacking in foresight and easily tricked'. This is clearly not true of the work of the comic playwright Terence (see above), but is more applicable to the Roman dramatist Plautus (c. 254–184 BC): his old men were constantly being tricked out of money by their slaves, or falling in love with young girls or courtesans set on fleecing them. One father said he was crazy for his son's girl, and felt like a boy of seven who had just learned his first letters of the alphabet – 'A'-'M'-'O'! (Latin for 'I love').

But Plautus' fathers could also be understanding of the follies of their sons (because they were like that too when they were young): strict in condemning their sons for their escapades with women, but only in their sons' interests, as their sons often acknowledged; and cooperative with other old men who had got into some sort of trouble, amorous or otherwise. In other words, they could have wider, more sympathetic, roles in the plots than merely as the butts of jokes. That raises the question of the connection between comedy and real life.

LIFE IMITATING COMEDY

If Roman comedy by its very nature took life to extremes to get laughs, it still drew on the circumstances of ordinary Roman life, however exaggerated, for its subject matter. It would not have been funny if it did not shadow real life at one level or another. Here Plautus made comedy out of a situation familiar, as it will emerge, to Pliny the Younger.

Comedy

The son of the old man Philoxenus has fallen in love with a whore. The son's tutor Lydus is absolutely furious and challenges Philoxenus to come up with a stern response:

> **Philoxenus**: Steady on, now, Lydus: the wise man controls his
> temper. It's less surprising if a young man does *not* behave
> like that than if he does. I was the same when I was young.
>
> **Lydus**: This over-indulgence has ruined him! But for you, I
> would have brought him up as a straight-living young man.
> But because you've been so tolerant with him, he's been
> thoroughly debauched.
>
> **Philoxenus**: It's only for a short time that a man feels the urge
> to have a fling. He'll soon start to regret it. Let him do it his
> way. As long as he's careful not to go too far, let him be.
>
> **Lydus**: Not while I'm still alive will I allow him to be corrupted!
> Was that the way you were brought up when you were
> young? When you were a teenager, you couldn't move half
> a finger's breadth out of the house without your tutor. If you

were not in the gym before sunrise, your trainer would let you know good and proper . . . [more follows on athletics training] . . . When you got home, you'd be sat down by your teacher in your loincloth and if, in your reading aloud, you got a single syllable wrong, you'd be beaten black and blue.

Philoxenus: Things are different now, Lydus.

Lydus: Don't I know it! In the good old days a man could be voted into office while he was still under the watchful eye of his tutor. But now, before the boy is seven, if you lay a finger on him, he'll hit you over the head with his writing tablet; and when you complain to his father, he'll say to his son, 'That's my boy, defending yourself against abuse!' And then the father will summon the tutor and say, 'Hey, you worthless old git, don't you touch my son for showing a bit of spirit!' . . . Can a teacher exert any authority under such conditions, when he is the first to get a thrashing?

All good comic stuff, of course – but hardly real. Or was it?

Life

In the following letter, Pliny the Younger (AD 61/2–112/13) lectured a friend on how to treat the young:

A friend of mine was thrashing his son for spending money too lavishly on buying horses and dogs. When the youth had gone, I said to the father: 'Come now, did you never commit a fault, for which your father might have reproved you? Why, of course you did. Do you not now and then still commit actions for which your son would equally severely reprimand you, if your positions were suddenly changed, and he became the father and you the son? Are not all men liable to make mistakes? Does not one man indulge himself in one way and another in another?'

I was so struck with this man's undue severity that I have written and told you about it, out of the affection we bear one another, so that you may never act with undue bitterness and harshness towards your son. Remember that he is a boy, and that you have been a boy yourself, and in exercising your parental authority, do not forget that you are a man and the father of a man. Farewell.

Cicero, too, was deeply embarrassed by his nephew Quintus, whom he had largely brought up, as he found him

the bitterest disappointment of my life. He has doubtless been spoiled by our indulgence, but I have combined humouring him with strictness, and I have had to put my foot down not over one fault or a small one, but many very serious ones. His father's kindness surely deserved affection rather than such cruel disregard.

THE PERILS OF FREEDOM

Cicero translated into Latin this passage from Plato, which described what happened when people power – Greek *dêmokratia* – was unleashed and normal human relations were turned on their heads. This was one of the Romans' greatest fears – a world without authority:

Homes are without a figure of authority – this even applies to the animals – so that eventually the father fears the son, the son flouts the father, all sense of shame disappears, so that everyone is free and there is no distinction between citizen and foreigner. Then the teacher fears and flatters his pupils, the pupils despise their masters, the young lay claim to the weight and authority of age, and the aged descend into the frivolity of youth, for fear of being disliked and censorious.

FUN, FAREWELL

There was no room in ancient society for the functionally useless: the sooner a child grew up, the sooner it could start actively contributing. The philosopher Seneca made a point of comparing children with adults who *never* grew up: children lusted after knucklebones, nuts and a few pence – adults after gold and silver; children played at being toga-wearing praetors and consuls – adults did this in real life; children loved building sandcastles – adults grand, important houses. The young, in other words, had the same basic affective impulses as the old; the adult, however, converted them from merely personal diversions into wider communal responsibilities – or should do. As Seneca elsewhere put it:

> We look on our infants and envisage them putting on the toga, doing military service, and succeeding to their father's property.

And it was this trajectory, as Cicero pointed out (p. 134), that laid the foundations of a good old age: the sooner you set out on it, the better.

Further, the more dissipated your youth, the less your chance of a happy old age (p. 126).

THE REWARDS OF STARTING EARLY

Consider the life tables: there were almost as many twenty-year-olds as there were those above twenty (pp. 12–13). They needed to be blooded, and as soon as possible. Given the chances of, for example, *not* reaching consular age, and even more of not living much beyond it, one can understand why elite families were so desperate to get the young into the race early. And the rewards for so doing lasted a very long time indeed. During the republican period, Roman families who had had a consul among their number were entitled to the epithet *nobilis* – 'well-known'. These families dominated the post to such an extent that, over any reasonable period of time, between 70 and 90 per cent of consuls came from a noble family, each new consulship adding yet greater lustre to that family history.

HOW NOT TO DO IT

Vespasian, who would eventually become emperor in AD 69, was a genial, relaxed, unambitious fellow. But he needed a kick-start and got it from his mother. While his brother forged keenly ahead with his own career, Vespasian made no particular efforts even to gain the quaestorship, which would at least ensure he became a senator. It was his mother, Vespasia Polla, who finally goaded him into doing something about it, 'not by entreaties or parental authority, but by mockery, constantly taunting him with being his brother's crowd-clearer', i.e. the man who went before a magistrate to make a path through the crowds for him. No wilting flower, she: indeed, *vespa* in Latin meant 'wasp'. No son sporting her name would fail to make his mark.

BRINGING ON THE YOUNG

A striking fact about the Roman elite is how young they could, if they so chose, start their careers. For example, from seventeen or eighteen, there were one-year posts for the sons of senators in the *vigintiviri* (The Twenty Club); four boards (originally six) convened to deal with legal matters, minting coins, road maintenance and so on. We hear of Cicero defending a client in the courts against a prosecutor aged seventeen! A few epitaphs recorded the careers of men dying in their early twenties who were already experienced pleaders and jurists (legal advisers). The same was the case with doctors: after a training begun at fourteen and lasting five years or so, there are a few examples of men who became doctors as not much more than teenagers. Politically, we find examples of young men aged seventeen to twenty-five holding positions of some, if not great, authority; for example, Pliny the Younger became patron of a small town at eighteen. Becoming a *quaestor* was the first big step, and this post at certain times could be held at twenty-four. Nero was emperor at seventeen, Commodus at nineteen, Elagabalus at fourteen. Admittedly, all three were disasters.

THE IDEAL STUDENT

Plutarch placed a high priority on education as the basis for the good life, and, therefore, the good death. He argued for the importance of the great myths and stories: they provided the means of introducing young children to concepts of right and wrong, and so to distinguish right from wrong behaviour. Learning was an eternal possession that would never let you down.

He urged 'university' students not to show off and try to win a reputation for cleverness by interrupting, or by casting unjustified aspersions and criticisms. If they disagreed, stay silent; let the speaker have his say; do not interrupt. Then come in with a question or observation.

Nor must they be swept away by mob admiration: keep the critical faculties open. In particular, beware of lecturers who were all style and no substance (Plutarch here told of someone who confessed he could not get a grip on a topic 'because too many words were getting in the way').

Likewise, a lecture was a performance in which everyone was involved. So sit upright, do not sprawl, pay close attention; do not frown, writhe about, doze, whisper to chums. Even if the subject matter was difficult to start with, stick with it. Most of all, ask questions if you did not understand. Showing off by pretending you did understand would do you no good at all.

U3AIN'T

Seneca argued with conviction that one's old age should be devoted, as Spurinna's was (pp. 81–2), to reading, philosophy, conversation and perhaps composing the occasional poem or treatise, combined with a little light exercise. But while Seneca was always in favour of learning, he was not so sure about *being taught* in one's advanced years:

An old man engaged in being taught his A B C [the Latin
elementarius used here derived from *elementum*, 'letter of the
alphabet'] is a degrading and laughable creature.

'Being taught' was for the young. Seneca seemed to suggest it was the
equivalent of being 'sprinkled' with knowledge. An old man should
be beyond that and already possess deep well-springs on which to
draw. Cicero, too, was rather sniffy about *opsimatheis* (Greek for 'later
learners', cf. our 'opsimath'). In a letter to a gourmet chum Paetus,
the ever-ascetic statesman said that since he was no longer involved in
politics, he had become something of an epicurean, so would expect
the full deal when he next came to dinner:

Prepare yourself! You are now dealing with a bit of a gourmand
who knows a thing or two; and you are well aware how pedantic
opsimatheis are.

That stern old Roman Cato the Elder (p. 103) might well have
disagreed with him. Though suspicious of Greeks ('an utterly vile
and unruly race'), he was said to have learned Greek in his old age,
and told his son that 'there is some benefit in investigating their
literature, but not in studying it thoroughly'.

SMASHING THE SYSTEM?

The modern world is used to 'youth movements', whose purpose is to
revolt, destroy the old ways and remake society in their own youthful
image. Is it possible to identify them in the ancient world?

The young could certainly be mobilized on behalf of a cause. Cicero's young friend Caelius was one such. He supported the revolutionary Catiline, whom in 63 BC Cicero as consul eventually managed to defeat. The historian Sallust talked of the attraction Catiline had for the young, but his reason why they were attracted to him had less to do with his deep-rooted political beliefs and more to do with hormones:

> But it was the young whose friendship he chiefly courted; as their minds, pliable and unsettled from their age, were easily ensnared by temptation. For in accordance with the particular passions he saw aroused in them, he provided whores for some, bought horses and dogs for others, and spared, in a word, neither money nor honour, if he could make them his faithful and trustworthy supporters.

This does not sound like a 'youth movement' in the way we might understand it – i.e. the young rebelling against everything their parents stood for in ways so fashionable since, for example, the 1960s. The youth joining Catiline resembled rather a bunch of young tearaways looking for adventure and tempted by the bribes on offer. The point is that, whatever way the young elite looked at it, the system was designed to put them on the road to success as soon as possible, and, as they looked back on their family's past, most would agree it had worked rather well (pp. 145–7). 'Revolution' against the old ways of doing things had nothing to offer them.

Chapter Three

THE DEATH OF CHILDREN

REJECTS

Recent analysis of a well excavated in Athens in 1931 and now dated to *c.* 150 BC found that the 450 babies discarded there – all but three were under a week old – did not die from a pandemic: a third of them, for example, had died from bacterial meningitis, an infection of the brain caused by cutting the umbilical cord with an unsterile object. Others presumably died from common conditions potentially fatal in babies, for example, diarrhoea. Such deaths occur frequently where hygiene is not a priority. In general, food and water contamination, poor sanitation and infectious diseases were the big killers. Even a small cut could result in inflammation and fatal sepsis. See further p. 66.

In the modern West, where the death of every individual, especially a baby, is held to be a tragedy, such mass callousness seems incomprehensible. But, for example, infanticide has been practised in many cultures over a very long time, and cultures tend, as a matter of course, to do what their ancestors did.

GOOD GRIEF

One common idea must be dismissed at once: that parents did not grieve over their dead babies. The 'evidence' for this is, first, that such grief is not mentioned in our sources. Why? Because so many babies died young that families must simply have become inured to it. Secondly, that the following sentiment, here articulated by Cicero, was common:

> If a small child dies, the loss must be borne calmly; if a baby in a cradle, one must not even lament.

The moralist Publilius averred:

> The death of a small child is fortunate, of a young man bitter, and of an old man, too late.

But all this ignores biology. The human race survives only because the desire for children is built into us, and so, too, therefore, is love for our children. Without that unconditional love, that inbuilt desire would come to nothing.

What Cicero and other Romans said on the subject related to the *public* – especially male – performance put on by the elite, whose 'duty' it was to set a good, solid Roman example on how to deal with disappointments. What went on behind closed doors was a quite different matter, and occasionally we find out – because sometimes that door was opened, especially in epitaphs.

Amid all this philosophy, the poet Horace touched a human chord with this almost throwaway line about the dangers inherent in the onset of the summer:

When the first figs and the heat
Enrich the undertaker with his attendants all in black,
And every father and adoring mother grows pale with fear
For their children.

EPITAPHS FOR THE YOUNG

If the elite did not remember their babies or very young children, other Romans did. *DM* means 'To the Spirits of the Dead' (see p. 154). This is the youngest:

DM: Lucius Cassius Tacitus [set this up] for his son Vernaclus, who lived nine days.

Here are some further examples:

DM: To Lucius Valerius, an infant, who was taken away unexpectedly. He was born during the sixth hour of the night, a sign of Fate not yet clear. He lived seventy-one days. He died at the sixth hour of the night. O reader, I hope that your family may be happy. The burial plot is 2.3 feet wide and 2.3 feet deep.

Note the reference to the dimensions of the burial place. This was to try to prevent trespassers intruding into it.

A freedman and his wife commemorated their son as follows:

DM: Eucopio [a private name], who lived six months, three days, the sweetest, most delightful, most pleasant infant, who had not yet learned to talk; Terminalis, born a slave, and Sosipatra his parents, made this for their most delightful boy Lucius Curius.

The next is an epitaph of a daughter old enough to talk. In the light of her age, she would seem to be more of a normal candidate for commemoration than the above two:

> To Vettia Chryses, daughter of Gaius; I ask you, passer by, not to walk over the remains of the miserable infant buried here in the ground. She will be mourned whenever people remember how her youth was taken from her. She was born for no better reason other than that she now undeservedly lies here. Her bones have become ashes, and the daughter can no longer talk to her parents.

The father of Nymphe (if that was indeed her name) contrasted his daughter's beauty in life with her state in death:

> If anyone cares to add his own grief to ours, here let him be and weep with no scanty tears. Here an unhappy parent has laid to rest his one and only daughter Nymphe, whom he cherished in the joy of sweet love while the shortened hours of the Fates allowed it. Now she is torn from home and is buried, dear to her own; now her bright face, her admired form – all is insubstantial shadow and her bones a speck of ashes.

THE WORKING YOUNG

Epitaphs are also a rich source of information about free and slave workers who met their end young. The fact that they were mentioned at all suggests that their owners or parents valued them and were proud of them. We hear of Melior, a home-born slave and expert teacher of arithmetic, who died at thirteen; the silver-engraver

Valerius Diophanes died at eleven. The child entertainer Pandion died at five; three brothers from Rome, gymnastic entertainers, died (two of them) at five, the third at seventeen months. Sperata, Anthis and Pieris, girls who helped their mistress with her hair and clothes, died at ages thirteen, twelve and nine.

CONSOLATION

The death of a loved one causes an intense emotional reaction, but Roman philosophers regarded the emotions as dangerous to one's mental stability. As a result, when Cicero discussed how to deal with grief, he identified a number of approaches one could take towards it: to uproot it completely; to calm its excesses as much as possible; not to allow it to take over one's life; and not to allow it to affect other areas of one's life. So (quoting a range of ancient philosophers) he offered the following strategies: one should think of death as no evil at all; or not a great evil; or an active good; or entirely natural and expected; and of mourning, that it is neither just nor obligatory.

UNMANLY BEHAVIOUR

In a letter he had written to Marullus on the death of his little son, the philosopher Seneca gave a guide to the way in which one should deal with a friend's excessive grief:

> Marullus was reported to be rather womanish in his grief, so in my letter I have not observed the usual form of condolence: for I did not believe that he should be handled gently, since in my opinion he deserved criticism rather than consolation. When a man is

stricken and is finding it most difficult to endure a grievous wound, one must humour him for a while; let him satisfy his grief or at any rate work off the first shock. But those who have assumed an indulgence in grief should be rebuked forthwith, and should learn that there are certain follies even in tears.

And that was the point – self-indulgent grief had no place when a small child ('a fragment of time') was lost. Not that Seneca did not acknowledge the power of the emotions at first hearing the news of a death, or at the burial. That was when 'tears fall naturally', but (for a right-thinking man) 'by a process against our will'. It was the unmanly yielding to grief thereafter of which he disapproved.

DEATH AS RELEASE

Seneca also composed a long letter of attempted consolation to Marcia (a friend of the empress Livia, wife of Augustus) at the death of her son Metilius. The main burden of the letter was that life brought intense pleasure and intense pain; both had to be experienced, and death was a good thing, a release from suffering. That her son's life was too short was irrelevant: how short or long 'should' it be? And what horrors might life have brought him? And much else in the same vein. Seneca ended with a striking description of the cataclysm that would eventually destroy the world anyway, as it renewed itself to start afresh. What could be more comforting than the knowledge that the world was mortal too?

GRIEVING FOR SONS

Quintilian, the advocate of a remarkably child-centred education, had already lost his nineteen-year-old wife and first son, when his second son died. His letter on the subject survives:

> After these calamities all my hopes, all my delight were centred on my [second son] little Quintilian, and he might have been enough to console me. For his gifts were not merely in the bud like those of his brother: as early as his ninth birthday he had produced sure and well-formed fruit . . . I swear that I saw in him such talent, not merely in learning, although in all my wide experience I have never seen anyone like him, but also in his power of spontaneous application, to which his teachers can bear witness, and such upright, pious, humane and generous feelings . . . He possessed every incidental advantage as well, a pleasing and resonant voice, a sweetness of speech, and a perfect correctness in pronouncing every letter both in Greek and Latin, as though they were his native tongue . . .
>
> Child of my vain hopes, did I see your eyes fading in death and your breath take its last flight? Could I receive your fleeting spirit, as I embraced your cold pale body, and go on breathing the common air?* Justly do I endure the agony that now is mine, and the thoughts that torment me . . .

---

* In the natural order of things, it would be the son receiving the last breath of his father, not the other way around.

Have I lost you at the moment when adoption by a man of
consular rank* had given hope that you would rise to all the high
offices of state, when you were destined to be the son-in-law of
your uncle the praetor, and gave promise of rivalling the eloquence
of your grandfather? And do I your father survive only to weep?

Quintilian's emphasis on a young boy exhibiting all the characteristics
and interests of a middle-aged man, whose elite connections even at
this age and proposed marriage would surely lead him to the top,
might not appeal to us. But that is to miss the point: the purpose of
children was to follow in their father's footsteps (cf. p. 23). The more
potential that lay in the young boy for achieving that end, the greater
the loss to his father and the more excuse he had for expressing his
feelings and the depth of his emotional distress. The future of the
family had now been consigned to the past.

DEATH OF A YOUNG GIRL

In this letter to a friend about the death of the daughter of Fundanus,
Pliny the Younger exploited precisely the same themes as Quintilian:

I never saw a girl of a brighter and more lovable disposition, nor
one who better deserved length of days or even to live for ever.
She had hardly completed her fourteenth year, yet she possessed
the prudence of old age and the seriousness of a matron, with the
sweetness of a child and the modesty of a young woman. How she
used to cling round her father's neck! How tenderly and modestly

---

* Roman families did not adopt babies; they adopted adult males if they felt the
family would benefit from it – for example, if they had no male children or the males
they did have were less than impressive.

she embraced us who were her father's friends! Her nurses, her teachers and tutors, how well she loved them, each according to their duties! With what application and quickness she used to read, while her amusements were never carried to excess and never overstepped the mark. What resignation, patience and fortitude she showed during her last illness! ... The moment of her death seemed even more cruel than death itself, for she had just been betrothed to a youth of splendid character; the day of the wedding had been decided upon, and we had already been summoned to attend it ...

DEALING WITH GRIEF

Pliny went on to point out that time slowly healed grief, and consolation would then become a comfort:

At a moment like this, all the philosophy Fundanus has ever heard from others or uttered himself is put on one side. All virtues but one are disregarded for the time being - he can think only of parental love ... just as a raw wound first shrinks from the touch of the doctor's hand, then bears it without flinching and actually welcomes it, so with mental anguish we reject and fly from consolation when the pain is fresh; then after a time we look for it and find relief in its soothing application.

PHYSICIAN, HEAL THYSELF

In mid-February 45 BC Cicero's beloved daughter Tullia died in childbirth, her baby son dying a few months later. He was beside himself with grief, left his house and hid himself away in his villa about thirty miles south of Rome.

Writing in consolation, a friend used the 'dreadful times' argument, adding that even if Tullia had had sons, they would not have been able to rise honourably to high office in the current political situation. Further, he pointed out that Cicero should not imitate 'a bad doctor, who boasts of his medical knowledge to his patients, but cannot treat himself'.

By this time Cicero's first marriage had collapsed and the second was about to. Cicero replied by saying that his recent political disappointments at his loss of influence and authority could be endured because 'I had a haven of refuge and repose, one in whose conversation and sweet ways I put aside all cares and sorrows' – but now she was dead, that was all gone, and both private life at home and public life in the forum were equally distressing to him.

CICERO'S ONLY CONSOLATION

A friend wrote to Cicero about Tullia's death, taking him to task for doing nothing but complain, when a man of his intelligence should see how pointless that was. Cicero admitted that the only consolation he could find was in his books, 'on which I spend all my time, not looking for a lasting cure, but only for a brief forgetfulness of pain'. He wrote to his old friend Atticus:

> Here I do not talk to a soul. Every morning I get up early and
> hide myself away in a dense, rough wood, not emerging till
> nightfall. Solitude is my next best friend to you. In that state I

simply converse with my books [he was writing a lost treatise *On Alleviating Grief*]. This is interrupted by fits of weeping. I fight it as best I can, but it's a losing battle.

It may be significant that all Cicero's grief was for his daughter: he never mentioned the baby (see p. 54).

TULLIA'S SHRINE

Soon after Tullia's death, Cicero took the extraordinary decision to deify her by building a shrine to her, 'hallowing her with every kind of memorial that Greek and Latin genius can supply'. He commissioned Atticus to do the negotiations. A lot of correspondence survives about possible locations and costs, but in the event the shrine was never built.

Atticus disapproved of the whole idea. He was not the only one. In letters to Atticus, Cicero complained about censorious communications from friends suggesting he had had a mental breakdown. In fact (he went on), he had been writing a great deal, 'the most elevated means of distraction for my sorrow and the most fitting for a man of culture'. In another letter Atticus suggested his 'popularity and prestige' were being affected, and Cicero replied:

I've no idea what people want of me or why they are so critical. Because I shouldn't be grieving? How can I not? Or prostrate with grief? But who is less so?

GOING TO EXCESS

Clearly Cicero adored Tullia and wanted her memory to live for ever. As he said in a surviving fragment of his lost treatise (see above), if Greek mythological heroes could be raised to heaven, 'she too deserves the same honour and devotion, and I shall ensure she gets it'.

But this was all too much in the eyes of stoical Romans. What was one of Rome's most revered statesmen and philosophers doing, caving in like this at the death of a daughter, and even proposing to deify her? This was an absurd response to something as commonplace as a death in the family.

Chapter Four

THE TRIALS
OF OLD AGE

THE EPIC VIEW

Homer regularly described old age as 'hateful', 'miserable' and 'harsh'. These epithets referred both to the physical condition of the old and to the horrors that length of years might bring, in contrast to the sweet beauty and innocence of youth. The Trojan king Priam, envisaging what would happen to him if his son Hector was killed by Achilles, begged Hector not to risk it:

> Have pity too on me, your poor father, while I still live my ill-fated existence, since Father Zeus has kept in store for my old age a hideous fate, innumerable horrors I shall have to see before I die – sons massacred, daughters raped, bedrooms pillaged, little babies hurled ruthlessly to the ground and killed, my sons' wives hauled away by murderous Greek hands.

Last of all my turn will come after someone's spear or sword has removed the life from these limbs; and my dogs, turned savage, tear me to pieces at the entrance to my palace. The very dogs I have fed at table and trained to watch my gate will lie in front of my doors, restlessly lapping their master's blood. It looks well enough for a young man killed in battle to lie there, mutilated by a sharp spear: death can find nothing to expose in him that is not beautiful. But when an old man's dogs defile his grey head, his grey beard and his genitals, wretched mortals plumb the depths of human misery.

OLD AGE, SON OF NIGHT

The farmer-poet Hesiod, roughly contemporary with Homer, composed an epic on the beginnings of the cosmos. In it, the features that would characterize this world – rivers, mountains, trees and so on – were personified as deities. Night was another example, and Night gave birth to Doom, Fate, Death, Misery, the Furies, Resentment (Nemesis), Deceit, Intimacy, Strife and 'accursed Old Age', which was feared, another poet said, 'even by the gods'. In vase paintings, Old Age was depicted as a bent, emaciated old man. In some, Heracles was depicted beating him with his club.

MOCKING THE OLD

Ancient literature constantly contrasted the value of fighting men in their prime with everyone else, male and female alike, especially the very young and very elderly. These last, being the least valuable, were the most useless. As the poet Horace said, describing the sort of capacities that one would expect to find in characters in literature: 'The young act, men in their prime take counsel, and the old pray.' That was all the old could contribute, unless you wanted some fun. The historian Tacitus described soldiers attacking a city and 'dragging off very old men, and women almost at the end of their lives, who, though valueless as booty, could be good for a laugh'.

THE SATIRIST'S VIEW

Juvenal gave a devastating account of the terrors of old age and its mental and physical deterioration. He devoted his Satire 10 to an analysis of the vanity of human wishes, one of which was a prayer for long life. But what did a long life bring? An unrecognizably wrinkled, baggy, hideous face, limbs and voice all trembling, bald head, runny nose and toothless gums – just like a baby. Even the keenest legacy hunter (p. 74ff) would be revolted. No taste for food or wine; a limp and lifeless penis. And deaf as a post, so no point in listening to songs or visiting the theatre. More illness and ailments than one could shake a stick at – dodgy shoulder, pelvis and hip; failing sight; needing to be fed, mouth gaping like a nestling.

But worst of all, old age brought with it loss of mental faculties: no memory for names or faces; leaving no legacy to the family but all to a wheedling prostitute; and even if an old man did retain his mind, he had no option but to attend the funeral of those younger than him – children, wife, brother, sister. And all the time *complaining* that he had lived too long!

Juvenal finished off with a list of past heroes who had suffered that fate, including Priam, the last king of Troy, who lived long enough to see the destruction of Troy and all its people (p. 57).

THE SATIRIST CONCLUDES: THE MEN'S SAUNA

Juvenal's recipe for a good life was: if you must pray for something, pray for a *mens sana in corpore sano*, 'a healthy mind in a healthy body', fearlessness in the face of death, an ability to endure sorrow, proof against anger, and a craving for nothing. Finally:

> So if you want a tranquil life, pray to be good. Lady Luck has nothing to offer – it is we who make her a divinity and set her in heaven.

SEX IN OLD AGE

Many ancient writers expressed disgust at the sexual activities of the old, especially when the young (usually a woman) and the old (usually a man) got together. The moralistic Plutarch was shocked that the even sterner moralist Cato the Elder (see p. 103), as a widower at the age of nearly eighty, was caught by his son in bed with a slave girl (who liked to make too much of a performance of entering his bedroom). Cato then went on to propose marriage to the young daughter of one of his under-secretaries. Her father was amazed: not only was Cato (he assumed) past it, but also, as an ex-consul who had celebrated a triumph, far too grand an eminence for any daughter of his. But he somehow got over the shock quite quickly and was thrilled to hand her over (contrast Cephalus on p. 122). A son was the result.

OLDER COURTESANS

Since the female function was primarily sexual, the providers of such services *outside* marriage were the subject of the most vitriolic abuse when their beauty faded. In their youth they exerted a mesmeric control over men. But when they had outlived their usefulness, males ensured they paid the price, describing them as still gasping for sex but now repulsive to men, despite their desperate efforts to appear young and desirable. This extract from a poem by Horace gives the general idea:

> You dare to ask me, you decrepit, stinking slut,
> what makes me impotent?
> And you with blackened teeth, and so advanced
> In age that wrinkles plough your forehead,
> your raw and filthy arsehole gaping like a cow's
> between your wizened buttocks.
>
> (tr. David West)

In another assault Horace described how 'the powdered chalk/and crocodile-shit dye run on her face as she ruts away'.

None of this is surprising. These women were seen as objects of nothing but male sexual pleasure. When they no longer provided it, they were seen as fair game for venomous retribution.

That said, Lais, the most famous courtesan of all, attracted moving epigrams on her lost looks: she whose proud beauty mocked all Greece, attracting swarms of young men to her doors, eventually dedicated her mirror to Aphrodite: 'For I have no desire to see myself as I am, and cannot see myself as I was.' Ovid, however, saw great possibilities in the older woman and gave useful tips about how she could maintain her physical attraction (but don't let your lover see all the jars and bottles on the table, and don't plaster it on too thick).

OLDER MARRIEDS

The married relationship was in principle deeply respected in the ancient world. Epitaphs spoke eloquently of what was at stake in marriage: love and concord into old age (see p. 157ff). Seneca, for example, expressed his concern for the anguish he was causing his young (second) wife when he decided to leave for his villa in the countryside in order to shake off a fever. He agreed that, since he could not ask his wife to love him any more valiantly than she did, he had to yield to her wishes that in old age he look after himself more carefully:

> He who does not value his wife, or his friend, highly enough to linger longer in life – he who obstinately persists in dying – cares only for his own comforts . . . although the greatest advantage of old age is being less concerned about self-preservation and living life more adventurously, one should look after oneself more carefully if that is pleasing, useful or desirable to one of your own.

Ovid told the charming story of two oldies, Baucis and Philemon, so pleasing to the gods that they were granted any wish they liked. They asked to die together. And so it happened. One day they suddenly saw each other sprouting twigs and leaves. Calling simultaneously, 'Farewell, my beloved,' they turned, together, into two trees, both growing from a single trunk.

DISEASES OF THE OLD

Hippocrates listed the following conditions to which the old were susceptible:

> In older people there occur difficulty of breathing, catarrhal coughs, blockage of the bladder, painful urination, arthritis, kidney disease, dizziness, apoplexy, severe loss of weight, violent itching over the whole body, insomnia, watery discharges from the bowels, eyes and nostrils, failing sight, blindness from glaucoma, and deafness.

Celsus added dysentery and general looseness of the bowels; and other common conditions cited in the ancient sources were bad teeth, impotence, gout, indigestion, sciatica and so on.

No wonder Pliny the Elder commented that nature gave us no greater blessing than short life, since people who were wracked with serious mental and physical decline could scarcely be described as 'living'.

FRONTO FRONTS UP

Fronto (p. 2) died aged about sixty. A quarter of his surviving 216 letters mention his physical pains. Arms, feet, toes, shoulders, elbows, knees, ankles, hands, neck, eyes, groin, back, loins, side, spine – indeed 'all limbs' – had their problems. He mentioned gout, neuritis, rheumatism, sore throats, coughs, insomnia, colds, stomach pains, 'illness' and perhaps cholera ('I lost my voice, choked, struggled for breath; my circulation failed, I lost my pulse and became unconscious; my family gave up on me and I was knocked out for some time . . . ').

On another occasion he was 'confined to his bed . . . so crippled that I can scarcely bend, sit up or turn round, so immobile is my neck', and had 'of pains and infirmities rather more than enough and to spare'. No surprise, then, that he turned down the proconsulship of Asia, citing ill health.

THE CAREER SOLDIER

Under the republic, the army consisted of ordinary citizens serving as necessary. Here is one. In 171 BC Rome took up arms for a third time against Macedon, the original home of Alexander the Great, which now dominated the Greek mainland. A dispute arose about the terms of service, and a soldier called Spurius Ligustinus, a long-serving veteran over fifty, was given permission to address the tribunal. He began, according to the historian Livy, as follows:

> My father left me one acre of land and a small cottage in which I was born and educated, and I still live there. As soon as I came of age, my father married me to his brother's daughter, who brought nothing with her but free birth and chastity; except, indeed, a degree of fertility that would have better suited a wealthier family. We have six sons and two daughters; the latter are both married; of our sons, four are grown up to manhood, the other two are as yet boys.

Ligustinus' military career, as he summarized it, covered service and honours in Greece (from 200 BC), Spain (from 195 BC), back into Greece (191 BC), and further service in Spain (182 BC). He went on:

Four times within a few years I held the rank of chief centurion; thirty-four times I was honoured by my commanders with rewards for bravery. I have received six civic crowns, I have fulfilled twenty-two years of service in the army, and I am now over fifty years of age . . .

Twenty-two years was the maximum that the state could ask a soldier to serve, but Ligustinus was now keen to go the extra mile in service of the state. Livy commented that many veterans were happy to sign up again, because previous wars in Greece 'had made men rich' from booty and handouts.

Ligistinus had done very well for himself. But that raises the question: what was the survival rate of soldiers in *battle*? It is a very difficult question to answer. Perhaps 50,000 out of 86,000 Roman soldiers were killed by Hannibal's army at Cannae (216 BC). But death on that scale was very rare. One recent estimate is that in 'normal' circumstances there was about a 5 per cent mortality rate among those who won a battle, going up to 15 per cent or so if one was on the losing side. The Roman army, however, won far more battles than it lost. One scholar calculated that from 400 BC to AD 500 about 885,000 Roman soldiers were killed. Compare the First World War, in which around 880,000 British troops were killed, and 388,000 in the Second World War.

THE GIG ECONOMY

In the ancient world there were no such things as 'jobs' in our sense, i.e. with terms, contracts, conditions, holidays, pensions and so on.

Nor were there any such things as health and safety standards. There was just work, if you could get it – an almost universal 'gig economy', with inevitable consequences for standards of living (see p. 5).

DIET AND DISEASE

No Roman citizen could live on the regular handouts of grain: there was simply not enough to feed a family, and a diet of nothing but grain needed supplementation. That would be basically provided by, for example, olives, wine, vegetables (chickpeas, lentils) and fruit, with occasional fish and pork, and, if necessary, lupins, peas, turnips, acorns, vetch and salad. A blocked tunnel from underneath apartments in Herculaneum brought to light evidence for the consumption of emmer, millet, barley, lentils, apples, pears, dill, fennel, poppy seeds, garum, anchovies, sea bream, damselfish and horse mackerel. One could survive with that sort of balanced diet, provided one had the wherewithal to obtain it.

At the same time, Rome was not a healthy place. The doctor Galen called it 'this populous city, where daily 10,000 people can be discovered suffering from jaundice, and 10,000 from dropsy.' The Elder Pliny devoted a whole section of his *Natural History* to the 'unheard-of diseases' that the city attracted from its immigrant population. Overcrowding meant disease could easily spread. Low-lying areas of Rome were regularly flooded by the Tiber: subsequent contamination of food and drink, and absence of – and ignorance about – basic sanitation, all had deadly consequences. The area was a paradise for the deadly strain of mosquitoes. Tuberculosis, typhoid and gastroenteritis were common. These infectious diseases were the big killers and, given the social conditions of the poor, would have carried off thousands every year. For younger women, childbirth was an added serial danger.

THE WORKING MAN

Training was available for jobs requiring specific skills. While most Roman children probably followed in their father's footsteps, both free and slave children could train as painters, sculptors, stonemasons, engineers, architects, copyists (copying manuscripts), dressers, perfumers, launderers, actors, name-callers (the wealthy needed slaves to remember and announce the names of their guests), barbers, dancers and waiters. Epitaphs inform us about many of these jobs: boys worked as mirror-makers, gold- and silver-workers, accountants, bakers, mosaicists, shopkeepers; girls as maids, attendants and dancers in travelling troupes. Roman Egypt provides us with lists of apprenticeships under contract available to twelve- or thirteen-year-olds. They lasted anything from six months to six years. They included nail-making, flute-playing, weaving, building, copper-smithing and wool-carding. Weaving was the most common apprenticeship, but all of these apprenticeships involved skilled work.

None of them was without physical risk, but much more at risk were those without training or skills who went looking for casual work of one sort or another. One hears of contractors for day-labourers to till fields, and cooks for hire congregating in the food markets. Docks would be an obvious place for porters to gather, building sites for construction workers, and so on. The latter, both skilled and unskilled, were in constant demand, sometimes (it has been calculated) making up 25 per cent of Rome's workforce. Likewise, neighbourhood and family networks and membership of *collegia* (see p. 000) could open doors to available work. In the countryside, in Italy and elsewhere in the Empire (especially Egypt), farming on a scale from a personal smallholding to gigantic estates provided rural families and city-dwellers with food. We hear of the young working with poultry, in the vineyard, wood-chopping, tending animals, and so on. As one graffito said:

> You've had eight different job opportunities – barman, clay-worker, dealer in salted fish, baker, farmer, maker of bronze trinkets, retailer, and now dealer in jugs. Lick **** and you'll have done the lot.

DANGER: MEN AT WORK

While there was always work available in Rome, those living at subsistence level (see p. 5) would be under considerable physical and perhaps mental stress as well. Combine that with hard labour in all sorts of possibly dangerous locations in all weathers and the injury and death toll would, by modern standards, be very high indeed. Cicero could wax lyrical about farming:

> of all the occupations by which gain is secured, none is better than agriculture, none more profitable, none more delightful, none more becoming to a free man.

But that was the vision of the gentleman farmer with an agreeable landed estate, run for his own pleasure by his freedmen and slaves. Cicero bought seventeen estates in his lifetime. He does not give the impression of a man endlessly slaving away on them. This picture bore no relation to the life of unremitting toil typical of men working estates or the average farmer with his acre or two, whose capacity to make a living for himself and family, with a little bit over to trade at market, depended heavily on the vagaries of nature.

THE CARE HOME

In the absence of social services, the old were reliant on their own resources when it came to the end of life. This may not have been much of a general problem, given that very few people would reach sixty or above anyway (see the age statistics on pp. 12–13); though if ancient views were anything to go by, by some measures old age could be judged to begin in one's forties (p. 18).

However that might be, the home was the only place to which the elderly could look for help in their advancing years.

THE ATHENIAN ANSWER

Official state positions were open to any Athenian male citizen over thirty, the final selection being made by lot. But to have your name put into the hat, it was necessary to answer a number of questions, among which was 'Do you treat your parents well?' And so seriously did the Athenians take this that they actually legislated for it: the lawmaker Solon ruled that anyone who did not look after his parents (and, it appears, grandparents too) should be deprived of his citizen rights.

The later philosopher Hierocles, as well as clarifying what that care should consist of, made the point that this was a reciprocal duty that children *owed* to their parents:

> For our parents, therefore, we should provide food freely, and such
> as is fitting for the weakness of old age; besides this, a bed, sleep,
> oil, a bath, and clothing – in short, general physical necessities, so
> that they should never lack any of these things. Thus we imitate
> the care they took in rearing ourselves when we were infants.

Athenians were in general very protective of the family. Orphans and
pregnant widows still in the husband's home were also covered by
that law.

THE ROMAN MODEL

Aeneas, the founder of the Roman race, was described throughout
the great epic about him (p. 180) as *pius*. It meant 'devoted to one's
family, gods and country', but in an active, not a passive, sense. That
was a component of what it meant to be Roman. In the context of old
age, it was taken for granted that a family had a duty of active care
to its elderly, everything from economic support to a proper burial.

And that was where, for the state, it began and ended: for, unlike
in Athens, no law was passed to impose this duty of care for the
elderly on a Roman until quite late in the imperial period (second
century AD). The reason may be that the structure of the family would
automatically ensure the desired outcome. The *paterfamilias* would
probably bid farewell to life before he kissed his marbles goodbye
anyway (pp. 14–15); but if he remained fully marbled, he would have
the authority to ensure that he was looked after properly. The same
would be the case for his wife as well.

BAD HEIR DAY

Wealth in the ancient world lay almost entirely in land. A landowner could raise vast sums by (i) renting land out to farmers to work, or (ii) getting his own staff to look after the land, cultivate it and sell the produce. Together with financial dealings, that was the way most aristocratic families maintained their position and status in Roman society.

But it brought a problem with it. It was a general practice that, on the death of the *paterfamilias*, property would be divided up in such a way as to give sons and daughters a good chunk. But what happened if you had a large family? Over time, the estate would be divided into such small parcels that the inheriting family would lose all the 'clout' which great wealth bestowed.

So to ensure that their wealth was not spread too thinly, aristocrats kept the family fairly small. But that, too, was risky. Given mortality rates, it raised the possibility of not producing a male heir at all. And if that was the case, the estate would disappear with their daughters, because on marriage they would take their share of that estate off to another family in the form of a dowry. That said, a timely adoption (see footnote p. 52) could solve the problem.

In fact, in any generation, about 75 per cent of aristocratic families died out, to be replaced by new ones. So the *paterfamilias* had to do some smart thinking about whom he left the estate to and on what conditions – and his treatment by his family would surely come into his calculations, if he lived long enough to make any.

WHERE THERE'S A WILL . . .

Roman law dealt with the problem of possibly dodgy heirs. For example, if the *paterfamilias* did not fully trust an heir, he could hand his estate to a third party with instructions to hand it over to the heir when the heir had grown up and shown a degree of responsibility. A woman who was sure her sons would waste her estate could hand it to them as heirs, but with instructions to give the estate to a third party to look after until grandchildren were born. When they reached twenty-five, they would inherit it.

Again, death could always strike children at any time (it has been calculated that about one in six couples left no heir). So the *paterfamilias* could leave the estate to someone he trusted (for example, his wife) with orders to pass the estate on to whatever descendants did survive.

FRIENDS AND ENEMIES

St Augustine remarked on the paradox that 'while the dead man lies, insensible, under his tombstone, his words retain their full legal validity'. That is why the Romans, like everyone else, adored a good will, and why a 'difficult' family might have had some qualms when the old man's will was opened.

The reason was that Romans also saw wills as an essential means by which the social networks which a man had constructed in life – the life-blood of an elite family – could be duly acknowledged and assured of continuing after his death. As Pliny said, 'wills are commonly believed to be the mirror of the man', since the *paterfamilias* (being dead) now had carte blanche to reveal what he *really* thought about those who had fondly imagined they were his nearest and dearest.

Since everyone wanted to know what the *paterfamilias*'s real views were, the contents of a will were eagerly awaited. ('I hear that Sextus is dead. Let me know who his heir is, and when his will is to be opened,' said Cicero in a letter, one of many such requests.) Such final public judgements really counted. All this helped to keep the family on their toes.

This could get serious at the highest political level. Augustus was paranoid about the last judgement of those friends he considered he had helped – downcast if they did not praise him enough, delighted if they talked of him 'gratefully and piously' (unsurprisingly, elite families left him an average of 70 million sesterces *a year* in their wills). Contrast Petronius (pp. 85–6)!

PIGSWILL

St Jerome recorded that schoolboys used to fall about reciting the will of a pig:

> Mr Grunter Squealer the piglet has made this will. He called for his parents, in order to leave something to them from his provisions. To my father, I give and bequeath thirty modii of acorns [other relations follow] ... And of my organs I shall give and donate to the cobblers my bristles, to the deaf my ears, to the lawyers my tongue, to the women my loins, to the boys my bladder, to the girls my tail, to the sodomites my bum, to runners and hunters my heels ...

And so on. It suggests that wills could spread assets far and wide.

LEGACY-HUNTING I

A well-known blood sport in Rome was to identify a 'rich old man' or 'miserly widow' with no – or only one or two – legatees, work your way into their good books, and try to make yourself a legatee – the sole one if possible, thus snaffling the whole estate when they died. Such people were loathed: they were denying everything Romans believed about the connection between birth, wealth and status.

In a letter to a friend, Pliny the Younger vented his disgust at the antics of one Regulus, who had made a fortune through this disgusting habit. Among other examples, Regulus visited a sick woman, pretended to read her stars, carried out a sacrifice, swore on oath it was favourable and she would get better. She wrote him into her will and promptly died. Regulus 'accepts estates and legacies as if he was owed them on merit', Pliny commented.

LEGACY-HUNTING II

The image of the old man hassled by legacy-hunters had another side to it. Pliny the Elder argued that as the world expanded, men became wealthier, and were selected for positions of power purely on the strength of it. As a result:

> Lack of children put men in the highest positions of influence and power, and legacy-hunting became a most fruitful occupation.

In other words, the man with no heirs could call the shots, as people chased him for his money ('barrenness in a wife makes for cheerful, attentive friends,' said Juvenal). Cicero made clear what that meant:

The legacy-hunter has to talk to the old man when *he* wants, carry out *his* demands, follow him about, sit down with him, load him with presents.

For Cicero, that meant the legacy-hunter was effectively a slave. Seneca suggested it was even worse than that:

In Rome childlessness used to be seen as a disaster for old age. But now it confers more influence than it removes, and provides such a route to power that some men pretend to hate their sons and disown their children. In so doing, they occasion their own childlessness.

However, as Seneca pointed out, 'If a lonely old man changes his will, the morning-caller transfers himself to another door.'

LEGACY-HUNTING III: A SATIRICAL APPROACH

Satirists had a field day with the legacy business. The poet Horace (65–8 BC) imagined Odysseus returning home from Troy stony-broke, and asking the prophet Teiresias (p. 178) how to restore his fortune, 'because birth and ability, unless they are accompanied by wealth, are about as useful as seaweed'.

Teiresias suggested legacy-hunting. That involved seeking out the old, the rich, the frail and the childless, and making oneself indispensable to them. Ingratiating yourself with the vulnerable was the name of the game: flattering, pimping and 'advising' were all cards to play, catching them as one would catch fish with a hook or stalk game.

One particularly profitable service, Teiresias said, was to offer oneself as a personal legal adviser on the subject of will-making. Do well at that, and many others would seek your help. Even if your target for a legacy had a son, it would be worth trying to become second heir, especially if the son was poorly: he might die.

If your targets fancied themselves as poets, praise their work; if they were lechers, offer your wife ('What! Faithful Penelope?' protested Odysseus. 'No problem,' said Teiresias, 'one taste of the cash and she'll be like a dog with a juicy bone'). And if Odysseus succeeded, he must lay on a magnificent funeral at which he was a picture of misery – ready for the next victim.

Other writers took up the theme – send your victims presents, wipe their noses – whatever it took. Just let a rich spinster or bachelor catch a slight fever, said Juvenal, and temples would be bedecked with vows to offer a sacrifice of a hundred oxen if they died, or even better a hundred elephants, if one could get them. Indeed, a legacy-hunter would hand over his best-looking slaves, young and old, male and female – even his daughter – to get the estate.

Martial mocked one Gemellus, desperately pleading with Maronilla to marry him:

'So she's a real stunner?'

'No – a hideous turn-off.'

'Then how's she so attractive?'

'She has a tiny cough.'

Not many legacy-hunters would go quite as far as marriage. Becoming a gigolo would (they hoped) be enough of a sacrifice to earn the cash.

DUTIES

In the course of his adult life, a Roman under the Roman Empire might be obliged to fulfil a number of *munera*, personal and public duties (cf. our word 'remunerate').

The most obvious personal duty was military service (see pp. 64–5), but there were others. Sometimes these involved paying extra taxes on one's estate; sometimes performing tasks such as maintaining public roads and buildings, perhaps with a financial contribution as well; acting as a judge or serving in office, which would certainly carry with it a heavy financial burden. One such office was that of local councillor in a provincial town. They held office for life and eventually the position became hereditary. They collected taxes and – heaviest burden of all – had to make them up in case of default. Then there was maintenance of buildings, streets, walls, water supplies sewage, food supplies and so on. In the later Empire, more and more people attempted to avoid the imposition.

In general, exemptions (bar military service) applied to those under twenty-five and those over sixty, and later seventy, and to army veterans. But all these rules could be waived if there was a shortage of candidates; and those *munera* which made purely financial demands usually remained in place to whatever age.

BUT IF NO DUTIES . . . ?

It was agreed that senators could 'retire' from the Senate, if they so chose, after about sixty. But that moment – as for those carrying out other useful public *munera* – might have generated a sense that their time was up. So it might have encouraged them to carry on the good work in order to remain useful. That said, given the typical lifespan and the absence of medical services, the problem must have been one that very few people were lucky enough to have.

GALEN'S ANALYSIS OF OLD AGE

The doctor Galen thought good health was created by balancing out the hot and cold, and the wet and dry, elements in the body. Blood-letting, purging (i.e. laxatives or enemas), food, drink, exercise, baths and so on were the means to that end.

For medical purposes he divided old age into three parts:

the 'middle period of old age, called pre-senility, in which the old can still carry out civic duties';

'senility, of which people say, "When he has bathed and eaten, let him sleep softly"; and

'the age of the "grave man", as those who enjoy etymology call it, because he is obviously on the way to eternity'.

THE GERONTOLOGIST'S ADVICE

Galen said it was possible to help the old with a mixture of medical regimes (see above), but it was not easy:

> To take charge of an old man, safeguarding his health, is one of the most difficult tasks. This art is called gerontology. And this condition seems to be midway between health and disease . . . so [whatever we call it] we must understand the condition of old men's bodies, because, slipping into disease from slight causes,

their former health must be restored as it is for those convalescing from illness.

But by the third stage, Galen implied, not even his medical expertise could do anything to halt the way to dusty death. And for Galen, dusty it was, too, being due to drying up of the body and its organs.

Galen described a period of slow decline as an entirely natural process, which is still recognizable today.

DOUBTS ABOUT DOCS

Pliny the Elder was cynical about the effects of competition in the medical market:

> There is no doubt that all those doctors strive for publicity through some novel treatment, buying their fame at the expense of our lives. This is the cause of those awful diagnosis-competitions at the patient's bedside, with no doctor agreeing with any other, for fear of seeming subordinate; it is also the cause of that miserable epitaph 'I died of a surfeit of doctors'.

Plutarch reported the saying of a Spartan king, when he was asked how they could conquer the Thracians: 'By appointing our doctor as general, and our general as doctor.'

GIVING UP ON THE OLD

Not all doctors were optimistic about helping the old to survive. The Roman doctor Celsus remarked that medicine itself could keep only very few people alive to the verge of old age. Another, pointing out that old age was incurable, suggested a doctor should do what he could, but where there was no chance of success, he should protect his own reputation.

This view was commonplace. Doctors were in competition for business with other doctors and could not afford to be known for losing patients, as the famous fifth-century BC Greek doctor Hippocrates was well aware. He recommended that, when dealing with tricky multiple fractures in the old:

> One should avoid such cases if one has a respectable excuse, since the chances of success are few, and the risks great . . .

COUNTERACTING OLD AGE I: DIO'S PERFECT DAY

There is nothing new about believing that keeping fit is A Good Thing. But it was not just physical fitness but mental fitness, too. That, and a good diet (see p. 127), were at the heart of ancient medicine.

Some time around AD 100 the genial philosopher and historian Dio Chrystostom (aged sixty) woke up to an unseasonably chilly morning and was not, so he reported, feeling too great. So he got up, did the necessary, offered a prayer and went for a spin in his carriage. After that he took a stroll, lay down for a little, had a bath and ate. He then decided to spend the day reading classical Greek tragedy, and selected the myth of the Greek hero Philoctetes, as told by the fifth-century BC Athenian tragedians Aeschylus, Euripides and Sophocles. These he duly summarized and discussed. Very useful for us, because we possess Sophocles' version, but neither of the others.

That was almost the perfect day for an old man – a little exercise, a bath, a meal and then a workout for the mind.

COUNTERACTING OLD AGE II: SPURINNA'S MORNING ROUTINE

One of Pliny the Younger's chums was Titus Vestricius Spurinna, a Roman senator and consul. Pliny said of him 'there is no one whom I should prefer to take as my model in old age'. Pliny then described his routine, 'as fixed as the course of the planets':

> In the morning he stays in bed till an hour after dawn. He then calls for his shoes and walks three miles, exercising mind as well as body. If he has friends with him, he passes the time in conversation on serious topics. Otherwise a book is read aloud … Then he sits down and there is more reading aloud or preferably talk; then for a ride in his carriage, either with his wife (a model woman) or a friend. After riding seven miles he walks another mile and sits again or takes himself off to his room and his pen, where he composes charming, pleasant, light-hearted lyric poetry in both Latin and Greek. When it is time for his bath, he first takes a walk naked in the sunshine, if there is no wind. Then he throws a ball for a long, active spell, the kind of exercise with which he fights old age.

COUNTERACTING OLD AGE II:
SPURINNA'S EVENING ROUTINE

After his bath, Spurinna lies down before dinner, listening to readings from some light and pleasant book. All this time his friends are at perfect liberty to imitate his example or do anything else they prefer. Then dinner is served, often accompanied by the performance of a comedy, so that the pleasures of the table may be spiced up with literature. Even in the summer the meal lasts well into the night, but no one finds it long in such charming and good-humoured company.

The consequence is that, though he is now seventy-eight, his hearing and eyesight are as good as ever, his body still active and alert, and the only sign of his age is his wisdom. This is the sort of life that I have vowed and determined to take up, and I shall embrace it with enthusiasm as soon as my age justifies me in sounding the retreat.

Both these examples describe the life of a retired member of the Roman elite. Such a life would still admirably suit the retired. Poor Pliny did not strike lucky, however: he died in his early fifties.

FEMALE EXERCISE?

Not a lot is said in the ancient sources about exercise for women. Nevertheless, the soldier-philosopher Xenophon, in a most sympathetic work describing how the good husband should train his young wife in managing the household, gave the following tips that will ring happy bells with many a modern woman:

She should not sit about like a slave . . . but try to stand before the loom . . . supervise the baker . . . stand next to the housekeeper while she is measuring the provisions, and go around inspecting whether everything is where it ought to be. These seem to me to combine her domestic concerns with walking. Mixing flour and kneading dough are excellent exercise, as are shaking and folding clothes and linen . . . as a result she will enjoy her food more, be healthier and improve her complexion.

Chapter Five

FACING UP
TO DEATH

REHEARSING DEATH

Seneca saw death as an important moment of transition. He therefore
had little time for jokers like Pacuvius, governor of Syria, who used
to hold regular burial sacrifices in his *own* honour, with wine and the
usual funeral feasting. Pacuvius would then have himself carried
from the dining room to his chamber, while eunuchs applauded and
sang in Greek to a musical accompaniment: 'He has lived his life! He
has lived his life!'

MOCKING DEATH

Petronius, who was ordered to commit suicide by Nero (as Seneca,
too, would be – p. 89), did it his way, as the historian Tacitus recounted.
A hedonist, Petronius had been admitted into the Emperor's close
circle because Nero thought he was the very epitome of 'cool': if
Petronius said something was smart and elegant, it was. Inevitably,

Petronius was denounced as a traitor by an envious adviser to Nero, and arrested.

Petronius knew what was coming, so immediately cut his veins. He then bound them up again and chatted lightly with his chums – no stoic fortitude for him, said Tacitus. He listened to them reciting frivolous poems and light lyrics, rather than engaging in portentous conversations about the immortality of the soul (see pp. 105–6). Then off to dinner, slowly dozing away his life.

His will was opened and found to contain none of the usual death-bed flatteries of Nero and his court. Instead, it named all Nero's male and female bedfellows, listing every novel sexual perversion employed.

CICERO ON GLADIATORS

Gladiators were often thought to set a good example of how to die. Cicero enlarged on the topic as follows:

> Gladiators who are either desperate men or barbarians – what
> do they endure! ... When prostrate with wounds, they want to
> find out what the audience, their masters, require of them. If their
> audience is not satisfied, they are ready to lie down and die. What
> even moderate gladiator ever groaned or changed his expression
> or showed himself a coward as he stood in combat, or even as he
> fell? Or what one of them, once fallen, refused to offer his neck,
> once the order was given? So much can exercise, thought and
> habit avail.

When Cicero was murdered in 43 BC it is arguable that he showed a similar gladiatorial heroism: leaning out of the carriage in which he was trying to get away, he voluntarily offered his neck to the killers with the words:

> Come here, soldier. What you're doing is quite improper, but at least you can make certain that you cut my head off properly.

Others, however, drew a different lesson from gladiators.

SETTING AN EXAMPLE

In a long letter about being ready to die when the time was ripe, Seneca argued that we could not all die like Cato the Younger (see p. 100). Further, he had some doubts about whether gladiators set such a heroic example in the ring: he thought they corrupted rather than inspired the viewer, though they were at least reconciled to death and accepted it when it came.

Strikingly, however, he did see virtue in those who 'when they were not allowed either to die as they wished, or to choose whatever instruments of death suited them, snatched up whatever was ready to hand, and out of sheer determination turned otherwise entirely harmless objects into weapons'. He gave three gladiatorial examples:

A DEATH OF CONVENIENCE

There was lately in a training school for wild-beast gladiators a German who was making ready for the morning show; he withdrew in order to relieve himself – the only thing he was allowed to do on his own, without the presence of a guard. There he seized the stick tipped with a sponge, used for cleaning his dirty parts, and plunged the whole thing down his throat, blocking up his windpipe and suffocating himself to death. Now that really was the way to tell death to get stuffed! True, it was not a very elegant or graceful way to die. But then, what is more stupid than to be fastidious about dying?

A BESPOKE DEATH

Recently a gladiator, sent out on a cart along with the other prisoners to the morning show, began to nod as if sound asleep. But he let his head fall over far enough to catch it between the spokes and kept it there long enough to break his neck as the wheel turned. So he escaped life by means of the same wagon that was carrying him to his punishment.

DEATH THROE

During the second event in a mock sea battle, one of the barbarians took the spear he had been given to use against the enemy and thrust its length down his own throat, saying 'Why, on earth, did I not long to escape this whole farcical torment? I'm armed – why wait for death?'

Seneca commented that these men understood that dying was more honourable than killing, and if desperate criminals had such stuff in them, surely so should those who had trained themselves by reason and philosophical contemplation to face death.

DEATH OF SENECA

Seneca himself admitted that all the philosophical conversations and speeches in the world meant nothing when it came to the moment of death: then you would show what you were really made of. His moment of truth came when Nero ordered him to commit suicide. His first request was for his will, presumably to add some codicils. This was refused. Seneca, assuming that Nero intended to invalidate the will (cf. p. 92), consoled his friends in true Socratic fashion (p. 100f) by saying that at least he could leave them, as Tacitus reported it, 'the pattern of his life, which, if they remembered it, would win them a name for integrity and steadfast friendship', and he rebuked them for their tears.

> 'Where,' he asked again and again, 'are your maxims of philosophy? Why did you bother to prepare yourself against future evils by studying for so long? Who was not aware of Nero's cruelty? He murdered his mother and brother: all that is left is to do the same to his guardian and a tutor [as Seneca had been].'

He then embraced his wife and begged her not to join him in death. She refused and they both cut the arteries in their arm. The blood escaped only slowly out of Seneca's, so he also cut arteries in his legs and knees. Fearful that his sufferings might weaken his wife's resolve and the sight of her weaken his, he sent her into another room. He then called his secretaries and started dictating to them. Still alive, he drank some hemlock (see p. 101), which had no effect. Finally, he was carried into a vapour bath, where he at last met his end.

So: Seneca lived up to his own billing in the ultimate confrontation with death.

SPECTATING DEATH

The Roman doctor Sextus Empiricus observed:

> It often happens that imagining something terrible is worse than
> actually experiencing it. For example, it sometimes appears that
> people who undergo surgery or some other such thing can endure
> it, whereas those who are standing around them faint at the very
> thought of what is going on.

To that extent, death is probably easier for the dying than it is for
the living, as Seneca hinted above.

ACTING THE PART

The idea that life was a stage was a commonplace in the ancient world,
as was the idea that in a single lifetime one could put on and take off
many masks. It is no coincidence that our 'person' derives from the
Latin *persona*: 'stage mask, character in a play'.

Seneca was alert to this. He pointed out that most of us change
masks throughout our lives, but only the wise man played no part
other than his own, the one he was designed for or adapted to.
Elsewhere, Seneca enjoined:

> Like a story, the important thing about life is how it is played out. It
> doesn't matter where you stop. Stop wherever you want to, but just
> attach a good ending.

And that was the point. One was putting on a show for the whole of
one's life, and one's death was just as important a part of it. However
good a play, its ending could ruin it. So with a man. He should 'be his

own audience' (Seneca) and make sure he lived up – and died up – to the part he had chosen (cf. p. 97).

The point Seneca was making is that there were no rehearsals for the moment of death: we all had one shot at it, and that was that, and a successful shot depended on how we lived our life. When the emperor Augustus was on his deathbed, he asked those gathered round him to applaud him for playing well his part in the comedy of life.

SUICIDE: TIMELY ENDINGS

As a stoic, Seneca considered suicide commendable, as long as the circumstances were fitting. So he toyed with the 'right' time to end one's life. Here he went into lengthy detail on the subject, including the prospect of physical incapacity to act when the time came:

> Frugal living can bring one to old age; and to my mind old age is not to be refused any more than it is to be craved. There is a pleasure in being in one's own company as long as possible, when a man has made himself worth enjoying.
>
> So the question on which we have to pass judgement is whether one should scorn extreme old age and not wait for it to come, but end it by hand ... But we shall ask this question also: 'Is the extremity of life the dregs, or is it the clearest and purest part of all, provided only that the mind is unimpaired, and the senses, still sound, give their support to the spirit, and the body is not worn out and dead before its time?' For it makes a great deal of difference whether a man is lengthening his life or his death.

But if the body is useless for service, why should one not free the struggling soul? Perhaps one ought to do this a little before the debt falls due, in case, when it does, one may be unable to carry it out. And since the danger of living badly is greater than that of dying early, it is a fool that refuses to stake a little time on the chance of a great gain. For few survive unimpaired through a great age to death, and life for many consists of lying there, inert and helpless. How much more cruel, then, do you suppose it really is to have lost a portion of your life, than to have lost your entitlement to end it?

SUICIDE: TAKING ADVANTAGE OF THE RULES

The historians Tacitus and Suetonius had themselves served at the heart of government. So they knew what they were talking about when they told stories of men instructed by the Emperor to commit suicide. The question faced by such men was: how to make the best of a bad job?

One answer was to do it quickly. There were two reasons, both to do with the result of a judicial condemnation to death: first, they would avoid death at the hand of an executioner; and second, if there were a judicial condemnation, they would be refused burial and have their property confiscated. If, however, they acted before the full weight of the law got behind the Emperor's whim, they would be buried and have their wills respected.

SUICIDE: HOW TO STAY ON TOP

In 49 BC, at the start of the devastating civil war in which Julius Caesar defeated Pompey and became effectively Rome's first emperor (p. 104), Caesar wrote to two of his allies as follows, proposing a new policy. Given, he said, that cruelty did not work, 'let fortifying ourselves by means of mercy and magnanimity be the new style of conquest.' He went on to say that he had already captured and then released three of Pompey's top men:

> If they wish to show their gratitude, they should urge Pompey to indicate a preference for becoming a friend to me, rather than to those who have always been our bitterest enemies: it is their intrigues that have reduced the republic to its present plight.

This must have sounded very noble, but showing mercy to enemies was in fact to multiply your superiority over them. As Seneca saw in a discussion on the topic:

> No one has saved someone's life without proving himself greater than the one he saved.

In that light, committing suicide, when your enemy had made it clear he was willing to forgive you, was to throw your enemy's 'mercy' back in his face. That was precisely why Caesar's enemy Cato the Younger committed suicide, as the biographer Plutarch understood (pp. 105, 107).

REFUSING TO BE SILENCED

One way of getting your own back against the Emperor was to revile him in your will (see p. 86). Another was not to change your character as a result of the Emperor's decision, but to stay true to yourself to the end.

So Helvidius Priscus. He was an ardent stoic and regularly crossed swords with the emperor Vespasian about the independence of the Senate. When Vespasian ordered him not to attend a meeting, the conversation (we are told) went as follows:

> **Helvidius**: It is up to you whether I attend the Senate or not. But while I am a senator it is my duty to attend.
>
> **Vespasian**: Very well, attend but say nothing.
>
> **Helvidius**: Do not invite my opinion, and I shall remain silent.
>
> **Vespasian**: But it is my duty to invite your opinion.
>
> **Helvidius**: And mine to offer what I regard as an honest reply.
>
> **Vespasian**: But if you speak, I shall have you put to death.
>
> **Helvidius**: So when did I tell you I was immortal? You will do your part and I mine – yours to put me to death, mine to die without fear; yours to banish me, mine to depart without grief.

SUICIDE AS PROTEST

Tiberius succeeded Rome's first emperor Augustus. During Tiberius' reign, the historian Cremutius Cordus wrote a work in which he praised Brutus and Cassius – the lead assassins of Julius Caesar – as the last and best of Romans. The paranoid and insecure Tiberius jumped on this. Augustus was the heir of Julius Caesar: how could those who assassinated him be the 'last and best of Romans'? So he prosecuted Cordus for treason.

Cordus pointed out that, in fact, Augustus had himself respected Brutus and Cassius, in exactly the same way that both Caesar and Augustus had respected other Romans who had insulted them. After some more in this vein, he ended:

> Posterity gives to each the respect he is due. If condemnation
> bears down on me, there will be no lack of men who will
> remember me as much as they remember Cassius and Brutus.

Cordus knew he would be found guilty, so he walked home and committed suicide.

The historian Tacitus, who recorded this incident, then commented that, although the Senate ordered Cordus' books to be burnt, copies remained hidden and were later published:

> So we should all the more deride the intellectual feebleness of
> those who imagine that the memory of later generations can be
> eradicated by today's despots.

Chapter Six

EXEMPLARY AND IGNOMINIOUS DEATHS

STAGING ONE'S DEATH

For a true Roman, male or female, the manner of one's death was as important as that of one's life. It was the last chance to demonstrate before the world the sort of person you had been (see pp. 90–1) – a cameo of the real you, the memorable climax of your part in the drama of existence. Here, then, are some famously heroic – and unheroic – examples.

The first is that of the Greek philosopher Socrates, offering a model of a death to which many a Roman aspired. This included the next example, Cato the Younger, the great-grandson of Cato the Elder, the most famous 'archetypal Roman' of them all. An anti-example then follows: the emperor Nero.

Women could die equally heroically: so Lucretia and Arria come next, and then a most unlikely heroine, a conspiratorial ex-slave, Epicharis. The section closes with Nero's mother Agrippina dying a defiantly 'male' death, and, the polar opposite, the emperor Claudius's third wife, Messalina.

SOCRATES

Socrates and the man in the street

Short, fat, with bulging eyes, thick lips and a snub nose, and a stonemason by trade, Socrates (469–399 BC) made his name in Athens as a bit of an oddball. He spent all the time, it appeared, asking questions about what goodness was and how you knew it was good. He used a comparison to make his point. A shoemaker knew what a good shoe was and how to make it. Who knew what a good man was and how to make one – and be one? Plato reported that a friend of his, one Chaerephon, had asked the Delphic oracle if there was anyone wiser than Socrates. The oracle had said 'no'.

This baffled Socrates, and to prove the oracle wrong, he went around asking various important and apparently wise people questions designed to illustrate their wisdom. But it turned out that they were not wise at all. So as a result of this 'cycle of [Herculean] labours', Socrates said that he was forced to admit that he was indeed wiser than anyone else, but only in this one respect: that he knew he was *not* wise, while those people he had questioned *thought* they were, when in fact they were not. This, he said, made him very unpopular, for two reasons: people who thought they were clever did not like being made to resemble prats, and the young loved watching him make fools of their elders and betters.

No ancient Greek liked being humiliated, let alone the pompous and self-important, let alone by an odd little stonemason like Socrates and his irritating young followers. Given that he appeared to encourage anti-traditional views about anything and everything, including the gods, it is no surprise that some Athenians were out to get him, especially at a time when Athens had been defeated by Sparta after a debilitating war of nearly thirty years. This may have created an atmosphere in which some Athenians felt a guilty party had to be found.

Socrates in the dock

In 399 BC Socrates was brought to court on the following charge: 'Socrates is guilty of refusing to recognize the gods recognized by the state and introducing other, new divinities. He is also guilty of corrupting the young. The penalty demanded is death.' Socrates was found guilty as charged. He was committed to the state prison and executed by drinking the juice of what his devoted disciple Plato simply called a 'drug' (*pharmakon* in Greek).

Socrates' fearlessness

In his defence speech, as recorded by Plato, Socrates made a point of arguing that he did not fear death:

> To fear death is only one instance of thinking oneself wise when one is not; for it is to think one knows what one does not know. No one in fact knows whether death may not even be the greatest of all good things for man, yet men fear it as if they knew well that it was the greatest evil . . .

This perhaps is the point in which I am different from the rest of men, and if I could make any claim to be wiser than another, it is in this, that just as I have no full knowledge about the things in Hades, so also I am aware of my ignorance.

This however I do know, that it is both evil and base to do wrong and disobey a better, be he deity or man. Therefore, I shall never fear nor run away from something which for all I know may be good, but rather from evils which I know to be evils.

Socrates closed his speech by pointing out that death was one of two things: either a sleep or a migration. He described the possible advantages of both and concluded:

And you too, my friends, must face death with good hope, convinced of the truth of this one thing, that no evil can happen to a good man either in life or in death, nor are his fortunes neglected by the deities . . .

Now the time is up and we must go, I to death and you to life; but which of us is going to the better fate is known to none, except the god.

(tr. W. K. C. Guthrie)

The day of Socrates' death

Plato (who had been absent sick) reported that on his final day Socrates and his friends enjoyed a long discussion about the immortality of the soul, ending with Socrates' beliefs, which he agreed could not be demonstrated, about the nature of the afterlife (see Chapter Nine).

Socrates then went into another room, accompanied only by his friend Crito, to purify himself in the bath, thus saving (as he said) the womenfolk the necessity of doing it after his death (only a purified body could be buried). There his three children and the 'womenfolk of his house' (presumably female relatives) spent 'a long time with him', saying their farewells, before leaving just before sunset.

The prison warden then came in, said it was time to obey orders and take the drug. Confessing that Socrates was a most 'noble, brave and gentle' man, he bade him farewell and walked out in tears. Socrates commented on what a charming man he was and how kind he had been, and asked for the drug to be brought in. Crito suggested he should wait till the sun had fully set, as most others awaiting execution did, but Socrates refused, 'because I would only make myself look ridiculous by clinging on to life when it had nothing left to offer'. So Crito told the slave standing by to fetch the drug.

The final moments

Socrates asked what he had to do. The slave told him to drink it, walk around till his legs felt heavy, then lie down. 'With his unflinching, bull-like gaze from under his brows and no change of colour or expression,' Socrates cheerfully took the cup, asking if he was allowed first to make a libation to the gods with it (a common practice at drinking parties! This is a good example of Socratic irony). The slave replied that only the normal dose had been prepared. So Socrates, praying for a successful journey to the next world, knocked it back.

At this, the whole company burst into tears. Socrates told them to behave themselves: that was why he had sent the women away, because one should make one's end in a respectful silence. Then, as ordered, Socrates walked about a little, and lay down. The slave pinched his foot: Socrates said that he felt nothing, and the same when he pinched his legs, which were now paralysed. The slave said that when this reached his heart, he would be dead.

> The paralysis had reached his waist when Socrates, who had covered his face, uncovered it and said his last words: 'Crito, we owe a cock to Asclepius. Do offer it and don't forget.' Crito assured him it would be done . . . After a while he stirred. The slave removed the covering, and his eyes were fixed. When Crito saw this, he closed his mouth and eyes.
>
> This . . . was how our friend died, a man who, as we would say, was the bravest and in general the wisest and most just of all those we knew at that time.

The offering to Asclepius

Those who were ill would take themselves to the temple of Asclepius, the god of healing, fall asleep in his sanctuary and hope to wake up cured. Had Socrates been ill and was cured, but had forgotten about the promised offering? Or was it a witty reference to Plato's absence from the death scene due to illness, which Socrates hoped an offering could help to cure? No one knows.

The drug

The drug that killed Socrates was the crushed extract of the poisonous flowering plant hemlock (*Conium maculatum*). If ingested, it attacks the peripheral nervous system; a very small amount – seven or eight leaves – causes death by paralysis of the muscles that enable one to breathe. The brain is starved of oxygen, leading to heart failure. Plato's description of the sequence of events – from the slave's instructions to Socrates' death – matches the effects such a poison would have.

CATO THE YOUNGER

The ancestral connection

Cato the Elder (234–149 BC) was the key to his great-grandson, Cato the Younger. The Elder was the original Grand Old Roman, passionate about Roman traditions and values, suspicious of all things non-Roman (especially Greeks), ascetic and incorruptible.

Strict discipline was his watchword, and the family the centre of his life, which he ruled with a rod of iron. He lived a simple, sober, frugal farming life, dressed plainly and was a merciless soldier. He developed into a powerful orator and advocate, and an influential politician during a period when Rome, now master of Italy, finally defeated the Carthaginian Hannibal in 202 BC and began to extend its power across the Mediterranean. It was Cato the Elder who constantly called for the final destruction of Carthage (*Delenda est Carthago!*), which happened in 146 BC. The historian Livy said of him:

> Without question he had a stern temper, a bitter, immoderately free tongue, but he had a soul unconquerable by appetites, an unwavering integrity, and a contempt for influence and wealth. In his austerity, in his endurance of toil and danger, he was of almost iron-like body and mind, and his mind not even old age, which weakens everything, could break down.

A changed world

Cato the Younger (95–46 BC) exhibited many of the characteristics of – and stood for the same values as – his great-grandfather. Uncompromising and of violent temper, he was committed to the old ways of doing things. His incorruptibility, at a time when 'everything in Rome was for sale' (as the North African king Jugurtha had put it), was legendary.

But Cato the Younger lived during times very different from those of his famous ancestor. The Roman republic had been ruled (as Romans liked to think) since 509 BC by a successful cooperation between nobles in the Senate, holding the top positions of state (consul, praetor, etc.), and the people, voting in political assemblies and fighting in citizen armies.

But by 49 BC this concord had collapsed into civil war between Julius Caesar and Pompey. In this conflict, Cato was a ferocious and unrelenting enemy of Caesar.

The Civil War

In 48 BC Caesar defeated Pompey, who fled to Egypt, where he had hoped to find temporary refuge. He was murdered on the beach when he went ashore. But the Pompeians fought on, and Cato and Metellus Scipio took fifteen cohorts with them to Utica in North Africa to continue the battle against 'the tyrant' Caesar from there.

In February 46 BC, Caesar's troops defeated Metellus. Cato had not taken part in that battle, because he refused to promote himself (who had never been consul) above Scipio. But he did agree to take charge of the city of Utica, man its defences and make certain it did not go over to Caesar. When it became clear that the battle was lost, he oversaw the evacuation of the city's population.

The day of Cato's death

The evacuation complete, it was suggested that someone might go to Caesar to plead on Cato's behalf. Cato would have none of it:

> If I wanted to be saved by the grace of Caesar, I should go to him alone. But I have no desire to owe anything to that tyrant in return for his crimes. Indeed, he is behaving like a criminal in acting as if he had the authority to save those [i.e. me] whom he has no right to.

That sentiment already suggested what Cato had in mind.

Further, one young man, Statyllius, urged by Cato to leave with the rest, refused, desiring to 'do a Cato'. Cato instructed two of his philosophical friends to 'rescue this man from his swollen pride and align him with his best interests'. Later that day, taking a bath before dinner, Cato enquired if Statyllius had left. No, he was told: 'He remains high-minded and resolute and says he will stay here and do whatever you do.' At this Cato was said to have smiled and replied, 'Well, we shall soon find out.' Cato, his companions and Utican officials then had dinner, over which they discussed philosophical matters of freedom and slavery, among them that 'the good man alone is free, the bad are all slaves'. Cato vehemently agreed.

Reading Plato's *Phaedo*

After dinner Cato walked about with friends, then bade them and his son farewell 'with more than usual warmth', and retired to bed to read Plato's *Phaedo*. When he had read most of it on the immortality of the soul and death of Socrates, he looked up above him and could not see his sword. So he asked his slave to bring it. He asked a second, and third time, punching the slave in his mouth so hard that Cato hurt his wrist rather badly, and crying out that his friends were betraying him, leaving him defenceless against his enemy. They came in and pleaded with him not to kill himself; but he replied he could do that anyway – but what if Caesar burst in and he had no weapon? He dismissed them all, except for his two philosopher friends, and told them

> I have reached no decisions about myself. But when I have, I must
> be the one who is in control of the action I have decided to take.

A small slave then brought in the sword. Cato tested its point and said, 'Now I am my own master.' He read *Phaedo* twice over, and fell asleep. At midnight, he called his doctor to bind up his wrist and asked a friend to find out if the evacuation had been a success; he groaned when he heard that there had been a storm at sea.

The death of Cato the Younger

As morning began to break, after a report that the storm had abated, Cato stabbed himself in the guts. But the damage to his wrist resulted in a feeble thrust, which did not kill him. He fell off his couch and the noise alerted the company. Plutarch, our source, commented that they rushed in and were appalled to find him alive and with his eyes open, but covered in blood and with most of his guts hanging out. The doctor came in and tried to pack the intact guts back in and stitch up the wound. When Cato recovered and saw what had been done, he pushed the doctor away, ripped apart his guts with his hands, tore the wound further open, and died.

When news got out,

the people of Utica with one voice called him their benefactor, saviour, the only man who was free, and the only man unconquered ... Caesar, who had heard that Cato had remained behind in Utica, came hurrying on to find out what the man (whom he greatly admired) was proposing to do. When he heard of his death, he is said to have remarked, 'Cato, I begrudge you your death, since you begrudged me the chance of sparing your life.' [Plutarch, now commented] In fact, if Cato could have endured to be saved by Caesar, it would not have seemed to him that he had disgraced his own name so much as embellished Caesar's.

These two famous deaths – Socrates' and Cato's – differ only in that one was legally administered and peaceful, the other a violent act of suicide. They were otherwise both in their ways heroic, and both driven by rigorous, principled beliefs, unshaken by the best efforts of friends to dissuade them.

The next could not be more dissimilar.

NERO

Nero the Emperor

When the emperor Claudius died in AD 54, Nero (aged eighteen) was rushed on to the throne. Nero was not Claudius' son, however. His fourth wife Agrippina had persuaded Claudius to adopt *her* son Nero over Claudius' own son Britannicus. Nero, we are told, had Britannicus poisoned, just to clinch the deal.

Nero reigned fairly responsibly for the first five years, since Agrippina, who was well aware of her son's propensities, put him under the control of two advisers, including Seneca the Younger, a millionaire philosopher. But mother and son did not see eye to eye, and in AD 59 Nero (we are told) had her murdered. He was now off the leash and could turn his attention to what he really loved: the theatre, extravaganzas, spectacles.

Nero the showman

The Roman *plebs* simply adored the big displays (theatre, games and triumphs) paid for by the Emperor, and they were captivated by Nero. He threw himself into it all with tremendous élan, regularly performing himself at games and festivals in front of delighted crowds.

He put on four-camel races, staged elephants on tightropes, even put on a play about a burning house from which the actors could keep any furniture they rescued. A keen lyre-player, singer and charioteer, Nero competed at festivals in Italy and Greece (where he felt he was really appreciated), always being awarded the first prize. If Nero did not win military battles, he could nevertheless celebrate triumphs by staging massive 'victory parades' for his successes in sporting and cultural festivals. When the centre of Rome burnt down in the great fire of AD 64, he appropriated the land for himself and built on the ruins a vast 120-acre Golden Palace (an original architectural masterpiece), complete with forests, lakes and wild animals.

Wildly popular as all this was with the *plebs* – graffiti in Pompeii are full of praise for him – it was not a hit with the ruling classes. They hated Nero because he had little interest in running the Empire, demeaned the office of emperor with his extravaganzas and ignored them completely, wielding power in an entirely arbitrary manner. One can see their point. If our Prime Minister spent most of the time touring the world as a professional darts player, taking on all-comers and always 'winning' to the applause of adoring crowds, one can see why MPs and the civil service might begin to have their doubts.

Rebellion

In March AD 68 rebellion broke out among the armies in Gaul and then Germany, led by generals who fancied their own chances of winning the imperial throne. When Nero heard that Spain, too, under its governor Galba had rebelled, he at first laughed it all off and continued in his old ways, but then began to panic. His praetorian guard did not respond to his pleas for help. One even quoted the poet Virgil at Nero with the words: 'Is it really so hard to die?' Nero considered some options: throw himself on Galba's mercy? Get an official post in Egypt? Clothed in black, address the crowd and appeal for forgiveness?

Nero flees

Turning such thoughts over in his mind, Nero went to bed in the palace, and woke up in the middle of the night to find that virtually everyone had left – guards, friends, attendants, caretakers. But not his freedman (i.e. ex-slave) Phaon, who suggested Nero make his way to his villa four miles out of the city, nor his (castrated) boy-lover Sporus, whom Nero had attempted to turn into a woman and 'married', plus a couple of others. Shoeless, wearing only a tunic, wrapped in a dark cloak and holding a handkerchief to his face, Nero set off. The villa was uncared for. He struggled through the undergrowth and crawled on all fours into the villa via a narrow passage which the others had dug.

No hiding place

Nero's faithful followers told him to kill himself and avoid the abuse he would face if discovered. He ordered a trench to be dug and material to be gathered for disposal of his corpse. All the time he was weeping and saying again and again, 'What an artist dies with me!' The historian Suetonius takes up the story:

> While he hesitated, a letter was brought to Phaon by a runner. Nero snatched it from his hand and read that he had been pronounced a public enemy by the Senate; there was a search party out for him; he would be punished in the ancient fashion. He asked what that would mean. When he learned that the criminal was stripped naked, his neck fixed in a fork, and then beaten to death with rods, he was overcome with terror and grabbed two daggers he had

brought with him. He felt the point of each, and then put them down, using the excuse that the fatal hour had not yet come.

At one moment Nero would beg Sporus to begin to lament and wail (Note: as was the custom with wives), at another he would suggest someone else should commit suicide, too, to set him an example. At the same time, Nero reproached himself for his dithering, as follows: 'My life is shameful, a disgrace – this is not the way for a Nero to behave, not the way at all – one should not hesitate at times like this – come, get on with it!'

The death of Nero

By now the horsemen were approaching with orders to take Nero alive. Realizing this, he declaimed, trembling: 'The thunder of fast-approaching horses echoes round my ears' (Note: this is a quote from Homer), and, with the help of his private secretary Epaphroditus, Emperor Nero drove a dagger into his throat. He was all but dead when a centurion rushed in and pressed a cloak to the wound, as if he had come to help him. Nero merely said: 'Too late' and 'So this is loyalty!' With these words he was gone, his staring eyes bulging, to the terror and awe of all who witnessed it.

Nero from hero to zero

What a shambles! Hardly the ending of an 'artist' at all, let alone an emperor. The man who had brought shame upon that mighty office with his passion for performing in public shows before adoring crowds might have reckoned on an equally glorious show at his death. But he could not even work up a noble suicide. Instead, swamped in self-pity, he died a humiliating death which he could finalize only with the help of his secretary, with no more valiant an aim than to avoid an even more humiliating public execution.

A constant theme in the Roman historians of the Empire was the extent to which the corruption of the emperors infected everyone around them – the fish rotting from the head down, in the old cliché (not that it actually does). Whatever glory Nero might have enjoyed during his life was extinguished by his ignominious exit.

LUCRETIA

In 509 BC Rome was still a monarchy, under the control of the seventh king Tarquinius Superbus – Tarquin the Arrogant. The clue to his reign was in the epithet. That arrogance was to be demonstrated by his son Sextus in his dealings with the noble Roman woman Lucretia. It would bring about Tarquinius' downfall, and with him the whole monarchical system, as later Romans believed. The story was composed by the Roman historian Livy.

Fun and games

Rome was besieging the town of Ardea. During a pause in the action a group of young noblemen was doing what came naturally: drinking, laying bets and so on. A discussion arose about who had the best wife, when Collatinus pointed out that there was no point in arguing about it: all they had to do was ride off back to Rome and see what their wives were doing. This struck them as a terrific wheeze. There being no laws about drunken galloping, they mounted horse and rode off, arriving in Rome just as night was falling (it was twenty miles to Rome, and a further nine miles to Collatia).

All the other women were whiling away the time with chums in luxurious feasts. But not Collatinus' wife Lucretia. Late though it was, she was still busy at the loom, working away by lamplight, surrounded by her female slaves. Clearly, she was the winner. She courteously welcomed them in and fed them. It was then that Sextus Tarquinius, overcome with lust at her beauty and chastity, decided to rape her.

The night meeting

A few days later Sextus dropped in at Collatinus' home. He was welcomed in, fed and shown to his room. When everyone was sound asleep, he made his way to Lucretia's room, held her down and tried to persuade her to make love. She refused, even though he threatened to kill her. So he tried a different tactic: unless she yielded, he would indeed kill her, but also kill one of her slaves, lay them side by side and say he had caught them in the act (death was the price of adultery, let alone with a slave). This threat conquered Lucretia's 'stubborn chastity' and she yielded. Victorious in his successful 'storming of a woman's virtue', he departed.

The morning after

Next day Lucretia sent a message to her father and her husband to bring a friend and come at once: a fearful thing had happened. When they arrived, she told them she had lost her chastity: 'the prints of another man's body, Collatinus, are in your bed. But my body alone is violated. My mind is innocent. My death will bear witness to that.' She went on to tell them what happened and to urge them to take revenge.

They promised to do so, but argued that it was not her fault: 'It is the mind that sins, not the body; where there is no intention, there is no blame.' She replied, 'I acquit myself of wrongdoing, but do not absolve myself from punishment. Never shall any unchaste woman live because of Lucretia's example.' With these words she took the dagger she had kept concealed under her clothes, stabbed herself in the heart and fell forward, dead.

The end of the kings

The others were overwhelmed by grief. But Collatinus' friend Lucius Brutus removed the dagger and swore on it that he would pursue Tarquinius, his wife and all his children, with fire, sword and everything else in his power to make sure that no king should ever rule Rome again. And so, eventually, it came about that the last king was driven out and Rome became a free republic.

Some 450 years later, it was to be Marcus Brutus, the descendant of Lucius, who would mastermind the assassination of Julius Caesar on the Ides of March in 44 BC. And on what grounds? That Caesar was determined to restore the monarchy. What went round, came round.

A woman's heroism

Vir was the Latin for 'man', and *virtus* (our 'virtue') meant basically 'what typifies a real man, manliness, steadfastness, courage'. It was displayed primarily on the battlefield. That was not a woman's world. Even in its wider meaning of 'moral excellence, goodness, merit', *virtus* was rarely applied to women. For in the Roman view, however contrary to twenty-first-century enlightenment, a woman could not be a man.

That does not mean that women did not have what we call 'virtues'. Far from it. But these tended to be the virtues that the good Roman wife and mother displayed in her correct place, the home, under the care and tutelage of her husband (p.158ff). And what could be 'heroic' under those circumstances?

Lucretia provided the answer in two ways: first, by her insistence that her fidelity to her husband permitted no compromise, whatever the circumstances. Replace 'husband' with 'Rome' and one could match such a commitment to the family with that of any soldier on the field of battle, where an individual death was as nothing if final victory was assured – as in Lucretia's case, she had absolute faith that it would be. Second, Lucretia's fearlessness in the face of death was the mark of a real soldier, and many a Roman hero.

This, then, was a form of *pietas*: that loyalty expected of Romans to one's obligations due to family, gods and state.

ARRIA

'Paete, non dolet'

Arria, the wife of Caecina Paetus, was a woman with form. Her beloved young son fell ill at a time when her husband was not well.

But she kept up the pretence that the son was doing fine, breaking into tears only when she was out of the room.

In AD 42 Paetus was charged with conspiracy against the new emperor Claudius. When Arria was refused permission to accompany him on the boat to Rome for the trial, she followed him in a fishing boat. Paetus was found guilty and ordered to commit suicide. But he seemed to be dithering over it. Arria took a sword and plunged it into her own stomach with the words, 'Paetus, it doesn't hurt.' Again, it is possible to see the same pattern of feminine heroism: unconditional loyalty to the idea of the family, and no fear of dying.

EPICHARIS

An unlikely heroine

In AD 65 conspirators planned to assassinate Nero. A former slave-woman called Epicharis, who, according to Tacitus, 'up till then had never shown interest in anything honourable', somehow found out about the plan and urged them on.

But when nothing happened, she approached a ship's captain whom she thought to be rather disaffected with Nero and suggested he join in. But she did not name any of the other conspirators. The captain reported the plot at once to Nero, who summoned Epicharis for questioning. But despite the lack of any solid evidence – one person's word against another, with no names having been mentioned – Epicharis was still held in custody. Nero rightly calculated that absence of evidence did not mean absence of a plot.

Torture

The conspirators' cover was eventually blown, however, and some, bribed with a promise of impunity, confessed. Then Nero remembered Epicharis:

> Reckoning that no female frame could stand torture, he ordered her to be put on the rack. But neither beatings, nor fire, nor redoubled efforts by her torturers, furious at being thwarted by a woman, broke her to confess anything. Next day she was dragged back in a chair – her dislocated limbs could not support her – for further torture. But tearing off her breast-band, she formed it into a noose, looped it round the chair-back and, by pressing her whole weight against it, squeezed out what little life she had left.

Tacitus' analysis

The historian Tacitus commented that this was a remarkable example set by a former slave, and a woman at that: freeborn Roman knights and senators were singing like canaries, he said, without a finger being laid on them, and here was Epicharis, enduring unspeakable torture to shield people she scarcely knew. Perhaps she was acting honourably at last, demonstrating a loyalty not to husband and family, on the usual feminine model, but to the idea of Rome. Or was it simply honour among thieves? But maybe that was better than no honour at all, at a time when corruption was so rife among real Romans.

Tacitus saw a degree of ambiguity about Epicharis' death, but there was no ambiguity about the death of Nero's mother.

AGRIPPINA

We have already seen how women could die heroically on their own terms – in the name of the family (pp. 115–16). Agrippina, the mother of Nero, came as close as any woman to a Roman ideal of male courage: fearless contempt of her assassins as they moved in to kill her.

A botched job

Nero had decided to kill his mother because he was tired of her attempts to control him (p. 108). He tried to kill her by means of a rigged 'accident' on board a boat at night, but it did not work and Agrippina swam to shore. As she did so, a female slave, thrashing about in the water, wanted to save herself and thought it would be a good idea to shout out that she was Agrippina. She was promptly beaten to death by soldiers. Agrippina saw this and drew the right conclusion. She took refuge in one of her nearby villas, but when news of the failed murder attempt reached Nero, he was appalled. Half-dead with fear, he sent soldiers to find his mother and finish her off.

A gladiator's death

The soldiers burst into the villa, and Agrippina faced them: 'If you have come to visit me, you can report that I am better. If you have come to kill me, I know my son is not responsible. He did not order his mother's death.' A soldier clubbed her and, as another drew his sword to kill her, she pointed to her womb and cried, 'Stab me here!'

It was almost as if she had expected it. Elsewhere, Tacitus reported that Agrippina had consulted astrologers, who had told her that Nero would indeed become emperor, but he would kill her – and (according to Tacitus) she dismissed this with the words 'Let him – as long as he becomes emperor!'

Here was a woman who, like a gladiator in the ring (p. 86), played to the crowd (in this case, a group of soldiers) and showed no fear at death, even telling them where to strike her.

MESSALINA

The libido-crazed Messalina, the third wife of the emperor Claudius, was a different case. She was said to have won a shagging competition with prostitutes and (according to the satirist Juvenal) served regularly in a brothel:

> When the pimp let all the other girls go home, she stayed as long as she could before shutting up shop, sad to leave and still on heat, clitoris rigid. Finally she got back to the palace, exhausted but still unsatisfied, and, cheeks filthy with grease, stinking of smoky lamps, she transferred the steaming fumes of the brothel into the Emperor's bed.

When Messalina secretly married one of her lovers, soldiers were sent to deal with her. Her mother begged her at least to die with honour, but all Messalina could do was weep and complain. When her assassin came in, she tried feebly to kill herself with a dagger, but all she could do was hold it to her throat and then her breast, trembling. The soldier drove it home for her.

Tacitus commented: 'There was no honour in that mind corrupted by lust.' Agrippina was no saint, but her end had been worthy of that fiercely determined woman. Messalina's wretched end, for Tacitus, matched her life.

HAPPY ENDINGS

It was not given to every Roman to meet, for good or ill, a dramatic end. That voracious encyclopedist Pliny the Elder took the view that life's 'greatest good fortune' (*suprema felicitas*) was to meet a sudden and entirely natural death. He produced twenty-nine examples, including Sophocles, who is said to have died of joy at winning a tragedy competition; and a mother who died after seeing her son, who had been reported dead after the battle of Cannae (against Hannibal in 216 BC), returning alive. Others died, for example, while putting on their shoes or after stubbing their toes, asking the time or eating cake, drinking mead, sucking an egg or making love to a woman, and 'two men of the equestrian order [while] making love to the same man, the mime-artist Musicus, renowned for his outstanding beauty'; while the 'most enviable case of all' was the comic actor Marcus Ofilius Hilaris, who, after a very successful performance,

> called during dinner for something hot to drink. At the same time, he took the stage-mask which he had been wearing during the performance and, while gazing at it, placed on its head the wreath which he was wearing. In that position he remained rigidly fixed, without moving. No one realized what had happened, until the person who was reclining next to him reminded him that his drink was getting cold.

Chapter Seven

CICERO'S *DE SENECTUTE*
'ON OLD AGE'

THE BLESSINGS OF OLD AGE

Romans were always looking back and drawing upon what they saw as the innate wisdom of Greek literature. Homer (see, for example, p. 23) and the subsequent lyric poets (700–500 BC) were on the whole pretty gloomy about the prospects of ageing and dying (and cf. the tragedian Sophocles p. 189). But the philosopher Plato began his extremely influential dialogue *The Republic* (*c.* 380 BC) with a discussion about old age between Socrates and his host Cephalus, which put a quite different gloss on the subject. This is how it went.

After Cephalus said how much he appreciated seeing friends in his advancing years:

Socrates: There's nothing I like better, Cephalus, than talking with old men. I see them as travellers who have gone ahead

of us on a road we too may have to go, and we ought to find
out what it's like – rough and difficult or smooth and easy.
I'd very much like to get your view of this, since you're now
at the time which the poets call the 'threshold of old age'. Is
it a difficult time of life? What do you make of it?

Cephalus: Right, Socrates, this is what I at any rate think. Men
of my age flock together, like birds of a feather, in the old
saying; and most of us get together to grumble about old
age, longing for the pleasures of youth, but now – no sex,
no parties, no drinking, none of that sort of stuff any more
– and moaning at the good times when we were really alive,
unlike now. Others bleat about how their relatives treat old
age like dirt, and sing it up as the cause of every ill.

But in my opinion, Socrates, they're blaming the wrong
thing. The point is this: if old age were the cause, I and
every other old man would feel the same. But as it is, I've
met others who feel about it as I do. Take [the famous Greek
tragedian] Sophocles: I was with him when someone asked
him 'How's the sex-life, Sophocles? Can you still get off
with a woman?' 'Away, man!' he replied. 'I was very happy
to escape from all that, like a slave doing a runner from a
raging, uncontrollable tyrant.'

That seemed to me to have been very well said at the time,
and I still think so. There's a great deal of peace and freedom
about old age when all that sort of thing is over. When desires
stop stretching you to bursting and ease up, you are freed, as
Sophocles said, from a host of deranged tyrants.

The fact is, Socrates, that these regrets, and also the problems with one's relations, can be attributed to one and the same cause – not old age, but a man's character. A man who is self-disciplined and good-tempered won't find old age a burden. For a man who is neither, youth will be just as hard to handle as old age.

Socrates then wondered whether it was Cephalus' wealth that in fact made all the difference. Cephalus did not wholly disagree, but pointed out one particular advantage of it: that when death approached, a man started to feel worried and fearful about the afterlife and its punishments, and began working out whether he had wronged anyone. But money played a big part in ensuring that one did not unwittingly cheat or lie to someone, or leave this life owing an offering to a god or a debt to a man.

ON OLD AGE: OPENING REMARKS

Cicero's dialogue *On Old Age* is, in a sense, an extended reflection on this key passage in Plato's *Republic*. The main speaker, Cato the Elder (p. 103), apart from summarizing much of what Cephalus said above, especially about character, went much further.

He began by emphasizing the need to lead a good and happy life within the confines of what nature allowed you to do. Since dying was one of nature's conditions, a wise man would face it without distress, as when 'fruit reached its full ripeness … and was ready to fall'. He cited a number of examples, including Gorgias, a Greek thinker from Sicily, who lived to be 108. Asked by someone why he had chosen to live so long, Gorgias had replied, 'Because old age gives me nothing to complain about' – an outstanding reply, said Cato, fully worthy of a wise man.

Cato then laid out the charge against old age, under four headings:

It calls us away from active work;

It weakens the body;

It deprives us of almost all pleasures; and

It is not far from death.

In the rest of the dialogue, he faced up to these charges one by one.

CHARGES AGAINST OLD AGE: I
IT CALLS US AWAY FROM ACTIVE WORK

'Active work', said Cato, was for the young and strong, but while old men's bodies might not be up to much, the judgement, experience and authority of the old were of the highest importance. It was as if the young men climbing the masts and racing along the deck of a ship were of more importance than the pilot, but his contribution was far more significant than theirs:

> Great deeds are done not by strength, physical speed or nimbleness but by deliberation, leadership and sense of purpose. Such qualities, far from being diminished by age, are in fact enhanced.

That was why the Romans gave the Senate the name they did – from *senex* 'old man' (one of the fairly rare occasions when Romans, who knew nothing about the principles of word derivation, got it right): only old men could demonstrate the wisdom and judgement that running a republic required (although see Aristotle's view at p. 27ff).

Stay involved

Cato admitted that age could weaken the memory, but that was only because it had not been exercised. In fact, soundness of mind depended on maintaining an application of one's energies to something of interest. Think of the Greek statesman Themistocles, who knew the name of every citizen of Athens. No old man has ever forgotten where he has buried his money, the date of his next lawsuit or the names of his debtors or creditors! Lawyers and priests did not forget their learning. Sophocles was still writing tragedies into his eighties. When his sons brought a legal case saying that he was incapable of managing his affairs, he simply read out in court a passage from a play on which he was then working (*Oedipus at Colonus*), and was immediately acquitted.

Such soundness of mind applied equally to those old men who continued working on their farms: they knew that next year they would see the fruits of their labours, but they also thought of future generations and looked to the long-term. As a farmer in the play *Young Comrades* by Caecilius Statius said, he was planting trees

for the immortal gods, who have wanted me not only to accept these things from my ancestors, but also to pass them on to my descendants.

Cato admitted that some people thought the old were bores, but he urged the old to cultivate the young, who always welcomed their experience.

So a busy life, building on the interests one had developed in earlier years, was the answer for a happy old age. As the statesman Solon said, 'I grow old, adding to my knowledge every day.'

CHARGES AGAINST OLD AGE: II
IT WEAKENS THE BODY

Cato dealt with this one by arguing from the example set by the famous wrestler Milo. Now an old man, Milo wept as he watched young athletes training; and, looking at his muscles, he remarked, 'But these are now certainly dead.' No, said Cato: *he* was dead, in the sense that Milo's fame derived not from who he was, but simply from his muscles. As a result – and this was the key – Milo could not accommodate himself to the new circumstances of his life, since life meant nothing to him without his muscular power.

In contrast, Cato mentioned distinguished orators whose lung-power might have diminished, but who had adapted (like himself) to a quieter and more relaxed style of speaking. However, if one could not manage that, then taking the young in hand was the next best thing:

> There are none who impart the liberal arts [meaning culture, especially literary culture] who are not judged happy, however old and infirm they may have become.

That said, age *per se* was not usually the reason for physical decline. That was normally down to an ill-disciplined and dissolute existence in adolescence.

Live your age

Complain as one might against old age, however, it was a simple fact, said Cato, that life had its own proper character and activities, and nature its one undeviating path:

As a child, you were weak; as a young man, self-assertive; in the middle years, authoritative; in old age, mature of judgement. Each stage has its place in the nature of things, for harvesting in its time.

For that reason, the old were not expected to remain vigorously active, said Cato. Indeed, the state relieved them of duties of which they were incapable (for example, soldiering and attending the Senate; see p. 77). Nevertheless, the old should fight against weakness and ill health where they could, and that meant a strict regime of moderate exercise and careful diet. If you became sluggish and dozy, that was the fault of your character, in the same way as youthful follies were the fault of the young.

Stay Independent

Strength of mind, not of the body, was what counted. A man devoted to mental activity and keeping his memory sharp ('my running track for the brain', said Cato) did not notice the advance of old age, so gradually did one's life approach its end. In the meantime, Cato issued a clarion-call for the old not to give up their independence:

Age is respected if it actively defends itself, keeps a firm grip on its entitlements, is subservient to no one and maintains control over its family to the very last breath.

The *paterfamilias* rules (see p. 14)! That, said Cato, was the sort of youthful assertiveness that he admired in an old man, in the same way that he admired a touch of the old man in the young.

CHARGES AGAINST OLD AGE: III
IT DEPRIVES US OF ALMOST ALL PLEASURES

Since ancient philosophers consistently inveighed against lust on the grounds that it tended to distort our reasoning faculties, it is not surprising that Cato saw the decline or loss of sexual passion to be one of old age's greatest blessings (cf. Cephalus, p.122):

> For where lust is the master, there is no place for self-control;
> under the rule of sensual pleasure, virtue cannot make any sort of
> stand . . . it impedes judgement, is hostile to reason, and as it were
> blindfolds the eyes of the mind, denying it any traffic with virtue.

Even less surprising was Cato's sideswipe against Epicureanism, which took a stand against normal philosophical opinion and 'asserted that everything we do should be judged by its pleasurability':

> When this doctrine was reported to the Roman generals [fighting
> the Samnites and then the Greek army under Pyrrhus], they
> expressed the hope that the enemy would be persuaded by
> it, since they would be far easier to conquer if they committed
> themselves to it!

It was not only the sexual urges that age diminished, but also the desire for excessive indulgence in banquets, parties and drinks. Result? 'No more drunkenness, indigestion and sleepless nights!'

Nevertheless, Cato did admit that for those who desired such things, it was frustrating to miss them; but for those who did not desire them, not missing them was a perfectly satisfactory outcome.

POSITIVE PLEASURES: I COMPANIONSHIP

Cato always enjoyed conversation, mainly for the companionship rather than the eating and drinking. As he pointed out, the Latin for such an occasion was not from the Greek *sumposion* meaning 'drink-in' (our 'symposium'), but from *convivium*, 'living together' (cf. 'convivial') 'because of its essential quality as a social reunion' (another accurate derivation). Cato said that he ate with his neighbours every day, talking on all manner of subjects and keeping going till well into the night.

POSITIVE PLEASURES: II KEEPING THE BRAIN ACTIVE

Since sex, ambition, rivalry and quarrelling were all things of the past, 'the soul has itself for company and lives with itself', suggested Cato, as long as it had knowledge and learning to feed off. He quoted the natural scientist Gaius Sulpicius Gallus, engaged day and night in 'measuring the heavens and earth', and others working on 'lighter' pursuits such as poetry and the law.

POSITIVE PLEASURES: III FARMING

Cato expressed his delight not only in the produce of the soil, but also in the workings of the earth itself. He emphasized the growth of corn and the vine, which he described in detail, cultivation (with its irrigation, ditching and hoeing), manuring, planting, grafting, and the sheer pleasure offered by cornfields, meadows, vineyards, orchards, cattle pastures, bees, flowers and so on. And this activity imbued men such as the soldier Manius Curius Dentatus with abstemiousness, self-control and a strong sense of values. When Sabine enemies tried to bribe him with a massive gift of gold, he replied that it did not seem to him that there was anything glorious in possessing gold, but only in ruling its possessors.

POSITIVE PLEASURES: IV
THE ENVIRONMENT

Much more in praise of farming followed: the satisfaction farming brought; the service farmers rendered to the whole human race in producing everything that was needed both for the sustenance of mankind and the worship of the gods; and the environment it offered for the old to enjoy: sunshine and the fireside for warmth, and shade and running water for coolness and good health. Here indeed was the true hedonism: the farmer, 'who has an account in earth's bank', always enjoyed a full wine-cellar, oil store and larder, abundance of meats, cheese and milk, and his garden, too, which farmers called 'their second leg of pork'.

> So let others enjoy their weapons, horses, spears, clubs and exercises with balls, hunting and running. They can leave us oldies our knuckle-bones and dice, though old age is perfectly happy without them.

POSITIVE PLEASURES: V EARN RESPECT

Then there was the respect in which old age was held. But it had to be earned, and for that to happen, its foundations needed laying early in life:

An old age that has to be defended by justifying itself is truly
miserable. Grey hairs and wrinkles do not automatically command
respect. That ultimate prize is garnered only on the strength of
well-spent earlier years.

Then, to illustrate how the old should be treated, Cato told a fine story
involving the Spartans. In Athens, an old man entered the theatre to
see the play, and not a single person made a seat for him. But when
he came to the section where some specially invited Spartan delegates
were sitting, they all rose to offer him one. At this the whole audience
applauded; at which one of the Spartans commented, 'The Athenians
know what the right thing to do is. They just don't do it.'

All that said, Cato did admit there was a downside to old
age: people accused the old of being hard to please, anxious, bad-
tempered, obdurate and avaricious. He agreed that there was some
excuse for this, in that the old felt themselves despised, looked down
upon and derided; nevertheless, it was primarily a fault of character,
not old age. There was a place for strictness in the old, though only
in moderation, but miserliness? Surely not: 'Can anything be more
ridiculous than a traveller needing *more* provisions the closer he is to
his destination?'

The conclusion of this section on that note led Cato naturally on
to the final charge.

CHARGES AGAINST OLD AGE: IV
IT IS NOT FAR FROM DEATH

Cato began by saying 'of course' this was the case and anyone who did not understand this was to be pitied. So he prepared the ground for a shift of the argument towards the question 'Is the soul immortal?' by asserting that there were only two options after death: either the soul was completely destroyed or it went to some place where it existed for ever, and *might* be happy too. In either case, there was nothing to fear.

Death to be welcomed

Returning to the inevitability of death, Cato pointed out that the young were far more prone to illness and death than the old (all too true: see p. 12). This he put down (absurdly) to the old's 'sense, reason and planning'. True, the old had nothing to hope for, but since their hopes had already been achieved – they had had a long life – that was better than an early death. Yet:

> In my view nothing is 'long' which comes to an end, since when
> that end comes, everything that has gone before vanishes at once,
> except your reputation for goodness and right dealing. Hours, days,
> months and years – they all yield. Once gone, they never come
> back. Nor can we predict the future. We ought to be content with
> the time for living that we have been granted.

Besides, Cato affirmed, everything that nature dealt out to humanity was good, and nothing was more natural than for the old to die. So he welcomed death the nearer he came to it, like a man approaching harbour and seeing land after a long voyage.

Cato then came up with another analogy, of nature dismantling what it had once put together, as if the builder were the best person to take apart a house or ship. And old buildings came down very easily.

Purpose fulfilled

Cato ended this section by repeating what he had already said about nature's plan for human life. Boys had their interests: did young men have the same? No, they had their own. Did those remain the same in the next stage of life? No, that stage had its concerns, which were not the same as those of the old. And as the interests of the old fell away, 'life which has had its fill brings in its train the proper time to die'.

The dialogue ended with some ancient theories of the immortality of the soul and Cato's final reflections, among which can be found:

> What benefit does life offer – or rather, what toil does it not? But whatever its actual advantages, its cup still becomes full, or it reaches its limit. I do not feel like lamenting my life – as many, and rather learned, people, do – nor do I feel dissatisfied to have lived, since I have lived in such a way that I do not judge I was born to no purpose. Further, I depart from life as if from a guest-house, not a home. That is what nature provides for us, a temporary lodging on our journey, not a permanent residence.

THE GOOD OLD AGE

Cato's monologue has at times a somewhat rambling feeling to it. He repeated himself, going back over the same ground in different terms, and would suddenly divert from the argument to make a fresh point which seemed to have occurred to him on the spot. Presumably this was intentional. Cicero was, after all, putting words into the mouth of an old man.

That said, there was a consistency about the recurrence of certain themes, which might be said to add up to Cicero's views about how to negotiate old age:

- Start young: the foundations of a good old age are laid in youth
- Be wary of putting too much store by material and physical pleasures
- Have a sense of purpose at every stage of life
- Keep working, especially on things that have always interested you
- Keep the brain alert: read, write and think
- Exercise the memory
- Keep learning new things
- Maintain regular conversation with friends
- Offer the experience of age to the young
- Enjoy moderate exercise, food and drink
- Stay as independent as you can
- Accept your limitations and relax into *being* old
- Acknowledge that it is a good thing that death awaits you.

Today, endless books bang on about 'the promotion of successful ageing', largely because the world of the technology- and youth-maddened twenty-first century resists the very idea of ageing. Cicero's message was: resist away, if you must, but much good it will do you. Raging against the dying of the light sounds all very romantic, but is about as useful as raging against gravity.

In the words of the old cliché: don't add days to your life, add life to your days.

Chapter Eight

DEATH AND BURIAL

I t has been calculated that about 30,000 died every year in Rome. Most were buried or cremated, but perhaps some 1,500 were simply tossed aside somewhere and abandoned. So death was everywhere. Martial described a man slowly dying by the roadside, flapping his rags to keep off the carrion birds.

POLLUTION

A boundary stone was found in Rome with the following inscription, ratified by the praetor on senatorial orders. It was a warning about keeping the pollution of the dead out of the city precincts:

> For the public good. No burning
> of corpses beyond this marker
> in the direction of the city. No dumping of
> ordure or corpses.

Underneath it was written in red letters:

> Take shit further on, if you want to avoid trouble.

The reason is that death was seen to be polluting, and the dead potentially dangerous in both a sanitary and a religious sense. So all cemeteries, grave-pits, funeral pyres and so on were set outside Rome's boundary walls, many along roadsides leading into the city. Tombs can still be seen, for example, along the Via Appia, where stood the monuments of great families such as the Scipios, Servilii and Metelli. But given the location, the stench of death would have wafted over travellers as they made their way into Rome.

THE BUSINESS OF BURIAL

For the same reason as above, the centre of the mortuary trade was kept strictly beyond city boundaries. As an inscription (here slightly modified) from the town of Puteoli made clear:

> Funerary workers must live outside the city. They must cleanse themselves after the first hour of night. They must enter the city only for the purpose of collecting or disposing of corpses, or carrying out executions, and must at all times wear a distinctive red cap.

Such workers (slaves were often used) could not take part in sacrifices or some public rituals. The trade was also suspect because it was designed to make money out of people dying ('What else do these people pray for?' asked Seneca). No surprise, then, that when one Horatius Balbus provided burial places at his own expense for his local community, he debarred 'gladiators, suicides, and those who pursued a polluted craft for profit'.

MOURNING BLUES

The Greek satirist Lucian (*c.* 117–*c.* 180) travelled all over the Roman Empire and left this account of a typical non-elite funeral, as suggested by the lowly career the deceased would miss:

The women begin to wail and shriek, and they all weep and beat their breasts, tear their hair and scratch their cheeks until they bleed. On some occasions they tear their clothes into strips and sprinkle dust on their heads. As a result, the living are more pitiable than the dead, as they roll repeatedly all over the ground and beat their heads against the floor, while the dead man, serene and elaborately garlanded, lies in lofty exalted state, decked out as though for a pageant.

What happens next is that his mother or even his father comes forward from among the crowd of relatives and throws himself upon the corpse. To heighten the drama of the scene, let us imagine that the dead man was young and handsome. The father emits strange and foolish cries, which would provoke the corpse itself to answer, if it could. In a plaintive tone, protracting every word, he says:

'Sweetest child, you are gone from me, dead, snatched away before your time, leaving me behind all alone and grieving, before you married, had children, served in the army, worked the farm or reached old age! Never again will you join in a festival or fall in love or get drunk at parties with your young friends.'

This is the sort of thing he will say . . . But the old man who mourns in this way with all the melodramatic ranting which I have described, and more besides, probably does not do it on his son's account, nor for himself. After all, he knows that his son will not hear him . . . it is on account of the others present that he talks this nonsense . . .

And that is the punchline. But whatever exaggerations this account might contain, it must have reflected some degree of reality if it was to be successful satire.

KEEP OFF!

Many funeral plots were quite large, and the owners feared that someone who could not afford a burial might surreptitiously use a portion of it. Hence the measurement of the plot and the warning:

> Here are laid the bones of Publius Octavius Philomusus, freedman of Aulus. Sacred to the gods of dead parents. Damage it not.
> Breadth 15 feet, along the road 15 feet.

Sometimes the warning was accompanied by the fine that would have to be paid if anyone infringed.

LESSER MORTALS

As the population of Rome grew, land became more expensive – and so did burials. Families that could afford it and wanted to offset funeral costs joined funerary clubs. Members paid a signing-on fee and then monthly dues, which were handed over at the monthly club dinner. One club had a joining fee of 100 sesterces (*ss*) plus an amphora of good wine, with monthly dues of five *asses* (1.25*ss*), for a guaranteed

300*ss* funeral. Anyone who defaulted on payments for six months got nothing.

The clubs also served as social clubs, with parties and feasts held in the club headquarters built above or next to the buildings holding the ashes, especially during festivals associated with remembering the dead (see p. 150).

The ashes were stored in an urn and placed in a *columbarium* (lit. 'pigeon nesting box, hole in a wall', from *columba*, 'pigeon, dove'). These were large, beautifully constructed underground sanctuaries, complete with stucco ceilings, frescoed walls, mosaic floors, etc., and fitted with rows of niches designed for the purpose. Many were decorated with, for example, rabbits, birds, dancers and general cavorting. The urns would be inscribed with a name, an occupation (if relevant) and perhaps a small dedicatory epitaph. One could buy a particular niche or take pot luck in a sort of Roman Urnie ('Lot No. 4, Place 34'). Committees were formed to oversee their maintenance.

THE STATUS OF FREEDMEN

Rather surprisingly, some of the largest *columbaria* – holding about 3,000 urns – were built for the Emperor's slaves and freedmen and their families. In fact, about three-quarters of the epitaphs found in Rome are for freedmen. This over-representation may be down to the inability of the Roman poor (the great majority of the people) to afford memorials of any sort (see p. 142, cf. p. 148).

At the same time, however, it is worth reflecting on what the citizen population might have made of the ideology of slavery in the light of (i) the Emperor's concern for the proper burial of his freedmen and slaves; and (ii) the freeing of so many slaves that quite possibly a majority of Rome's *free* population were actually ex-slaves or related to them!

EPITAPHS FROM *COLUMBARIA*

Most of them were very short and simple:

> Here lie the bones of Felix, bedchamber slave.

This one went into a little more detail:

> Within this place, the bones and ashes of Pinnia Didyma's good and pious soul having been positioned well are at peace. Titus Pinnius Hermes made this monument for his dearest and very well-deserving fellow freedwoman and for himself.

URBAN POOR

For those who could not afford any sort of burial, a simple reusable coffin-on-a-stretcher (*sandapila*) acted as a pauper's bier. The body would be taken to the pauper's pyre and thrown on to it. The satirical poet Martial described a huge Gaul who broke an ankle after a nasty fall at night while returning to his lodgings. His tiny slave (carrying a torch to light the way) could not shift him. So he begged four public slaves – who were carrying a poor man's corpse to the pauper's pyre ('one of the thousands that the pyre receives') – to help. Would they please load his master up on the *sandapila* and take him wherever they wanted? So the pauper's corpse was dumped, probably left by the roadside or thrown into a pit, and the Gaul took its place.

Pits (16 feet x 12 feet and 33 feet deep) have been excavated into which such corpses were thrown, with animals, carcasses, animal and human excrement and general refuse. One huge pit (160 feet x 100 feet x 30 feet deep) – in fact, an ancient moat – contained about 24,000 bodies. The stench was so revolting that the nineteenth-century excavators had to be given periodic time outs. The Tiber also received many corpses, the water 'purifying' the body while removing it.

FUNERAL DIRECTORS

An elite funeral needed careful coordination and choreography, and this was the job of the funeral director. He organized gravestones, processions, mourners, etc., as well as actors, musicians and singers. It is not surprising, then, that some were also involved in theatrical productions. The result was that, despite the polluting nature of the work, at least some funeral directors could have a standing in polite society; indeed, we hear of one Aprodisius whose epitaph revealed that he was both a funeral director and an urban official in charge of an important festival.

It is worth pointing out that the advent of Christianity changed all this. The body lost its terror as a force for pollution and became itself a sacred object.

THE DEATH SCENE

At the moment of death, the dead person would be given a final kiss, the last breath caught (see pp. 51–2) and the name cried out aloud. The women would then wash and anoint the body and wrap it in a shroud. A coin would be placed between the lips, and the jaw was tied up to keep the coin there, a payment to Charon, the Underworld's ferryman: it was important for the soul to be able to cross the river Styx or Acheron to the other side.

At this stage a death mask (*imago*) might have been made. Sometimes it was buried with the body; at others, it was kept by the family for display in the family shrine, complete with the record of the dead person's achievements. The body was then placed in the atrium of the house, and mourners, dressed in dark clothes, were invited in, including a man's freedmen. Incense would be burning round the body (to disguise any smell of decay). One could hire professionals to join in with dirges over the dead. A wealthy family might have had the body embalmed before cremation, though later in the Empire burial became the norm in Rome.

Because death meant pollution, a family was given an eight-day period in which to complete all the rituals before resuming normal activities.

THE DEATH MARCH

Unless the deceased was so important as to be given a state funeral, all expenses had to be borne by the family. The body was laid out in state on a bier and carried on the shoulders of the men of the family to the forum. There probably the son of the deceased would give a public eulogy; and then the body would be taken beyond the boundaries of Rome for the cremation. There would be the usual accompaniment of mourners, trumpeters, dirges and (the family hoped) huge crowds, as in a sort of triumphal procession (according to Seneca). At this time actors impersonating the dead man and his famous ancestors, probably wearing the family *imagines*, might be part of the procession: the whole family, past and present, was there. One can only imagine the impression that such a roll call of past heroes must have had upon the general public as they witnessed the history of a great family being literally paraded before their eyes.

CAUSE OF REJOICING

Whatever the close family felt about the deceased, there might well have been one part of the household for whom it was a day of freedom: the slaves, since occasionally the deceased would free some in his will. A satirical poet described them as 'day-old citizens' as they carried their patron out on the bier, the felt caps of liberty firmly attached to their heads. A cynical historian suggested patrons did this only to get a reputation as a good man and swell the numbers of the funeral crowd.

THE FUNERAL ORATION

Competition did not cease merely because a member of an elite family, male or female, had died: the family would ensure that the eulogy at the funeral of their loved one more than matched anyone else's. Menander the Orator (*c.* AD 300), who gave sound advice on eulogizing any subject, from a city to a harbour, suggested the following for a great man's funeral.

Encomia of the deceased, he said, should be based on the following topics: family, birth, nature, nurture, education, accomplishments, actions and Fortune, ending with consolation. Under 'family', the eulogist had to stress that there was none more brilliant in the city. 'Birth' was an important topic if a child had died: mention the rejoicing of the whole family, the splendid hopes, the prospect of a great destiny, all dashed by Fate. 'Nature' should cover physical beauty and mental endowment; 'nurture' should touch on the speed with which the person developed; 'education' should stress that he was far ahead of his contemporaries; 'character' should deal with his fairness, humanity, approachability and gentleness.

But 'actions', what the person achieved in life, was the topic that Menander suggested the eulogist should concentrate on, and he should point out that Fortune followed him all his life, so that he was wealthy, loved by his friends, honoured by the great and good, and so on. Throughout, Menander went on, the dead person must be shown to have been fit to rival any man in distinction.

But there was more to these rituals than merely celebrating the deceased.

PAST AND PRESENT

The historical significance of a Roman funeral was made clear by Polybius, a Greek diplomat taken hostage by Rome in 167 BC after it had defeated Macedon, then the dominant ruling state of Greece. In Rome Polybius grew to admire greatly both Romans and Rome's balanced constitution, and he wrote a superb history of Rome's battle against Hannibal. In the course of it, he digressed on the way Roman families celebrated their ancestors at funerals:

> The speaker, when he has finished dealing with the dead man, then recounts the successes and exploits of the other [great past

heroes of the family] whose images are present, beginning with the most ancient. By this means and by this constant repetition of the fine reputation of brave men, the celebrity of those who performed noble deeds is made immortal, while at the same time the fame of those who did good service to their country becomes known to contemporaries and acts as heritage for future generations. But the most important result is that young men are thus inspired to endure every suffering for public welfare in the hope of winning the glory that attends on brave men.

THE HISTORY LESSON

In these grand funerals, the family – especially the children – was being given a family history lesson, a reminder of what its great ancestors had achieved in the past, in order to act as a model for the behaviour of the present and future generations. The fact that the eulogy was being played out in public, in the forum – the very heart of Roman political life – made the occasion all the more telling: here was a family putting its cards – and its future – on the table. That said, the historian Livy did point out that the historical record was often falsified by families who 'try to appropriate to themselves the traditions of exploits and titles of office by means of inventions calculated to deceive'.

A GOOD LIFE

Aemilius Paullus was of a noble family going way back (the family angle was that they descended from Pythagoras). He had played the major part in defeating Macedon, the state that controlled Greece

(168 BC), and in turning Greece (with all its wealth) into a Roman province. Describing his funeral procession in 160 BC, Plutarch said:

> his funeral procession called forth men's admiration . . . not in gold or ivory or the most ambitious and expensive preparations for such rites, but in good will and honour and gratitude on the part, not only of his fellow citizens, but also of his enemies.

He then described how many of those he had defeated insisted on carrying his bier,

> calling aloud upon Aemilius as benefactor and preserver of their countries. For not only at the times of his conquests had he treated them all with mildness and humanity, but also during all the rest of his life he was always doing them some good and caring for them as though they had been kindred and relations.

That was the ideal: being a winner, but winning enemies *over* as well as conquering them.

TOMBS FOR PUBLIC USE

For the most part, terracotta jars, urns and slabs of stone sufficed for Everyman. But for those who could afford it, it was important to ensure that, when dead, they were well looked after and the general public would value them. Some people were so concerned about getting everything exactly right that they left specific instructions to their family. Here is an example:

My wishes are that the memorial shrine which I have under construction should be completed to the specifications which I have given:

The shrine is to contain a recess, in which there is to be set a seated statue of myself, made of the finest, imported marble, or else of the finest bronze, at least five feet in height.

Just inside the recess there is to be a sedan chair, with two seats on either side of it, all made of imported marble.

There are to be covers kept there, which are to be spread out on the days when the memorial shrine is opened, and there are to be two rugs, two dining cushions of equal size, two cloaks and a tunic.

In front of this monument is to be placed an altar, carved in the finest style from the best Luna marble, and in this my bones are to be laid at rest.

The shrine is to be closed with a slab of Luna marble, in such a way that it can be both opened and closed again without difficulty.

Some shrines were built to look like houses, with seats (as above) and barbecues around them, perhaps decorated with scenes from myth and daily life (especially dining, cf. p. 157). These would be for the family on family occasions, but also for any weary travellers who needed a rest. The deceased wanted their tombs to attract attention to themselves, as many epitaphs suggest (see p. 170).

FREEDMEN MADE GOOD

Such expensive monuments were not just confined to wealthy citizens. Those of freedmen could be even grander and more skilfully crafted, often featuring themselves wearing togas, with their families. Rightly, they were keen to stress that – from slavery and thanks to their technical ability and talent – they had 'made it' in Roman society (both Cicero and Seneca expressed admiration for the expert craftsman). Eurysaces was one such, a very successful baker: his gigantic monument (33 feet tall) featured three rows of four cylinders (kneading basins? Grain measurers? Bread ovens?).

SPECTACULARS

Tombs came in all shapes and sizes: altars, temples and towers were all popular. There was even a tomb shaped like a pyramid in Rome! But when it came to emperors, size went with magnificence. The mausolea of Augustus and Hadrian – vast circular buildings, dominating the skyline – showed what could be done. Further (and here we get to the nub) all had lengthy inscriptions. In other words, this was not just about a comfy death: it was all about impressing your contemporaries and ensuring a glorious future, where one's *achievements* would be immortalized and passed on to succeeding generations. But as Seneca observed, such monuments perished: he assumed only a written record would ensure the immortal memory of someone worth it.

REMEMBERING THE DEAD

Every year, from the 13th to the 21st of February, there was a sequence of festivals in honour of the family dead (i.e. the *di manes*, see p. 153), starting with the aptly named *Parentalia*. On the last day offerings were made at family graves, and then came a family get-together in which quarrels were patched up and families looked to the past and future. Meanwhile, on the 9th, 11th and 23rd of May a family's unburied dead (*Lemures*) were celebrated and appeased. They needed to be: malevolent, hungry ghosts, they left their locations at that time and returned to their family homes.

We hear of one Roman who left money to the relevant priests to make sure that on every festival remembering the dead, violets and roses would decorate his grave, oil would be poured into it (a little pipe inserted into the grave was usually provided for this purpose) and, to round things off, there would be a dinner with wrestling matches.

COMMUNITY DONATIONS

One could also be memorialized by leaving a sum of money for a building project or in support of children. One such donor had inscribed:

> And I wish the gift, which out of my generosity I have made
> to the gymnasium and to the city on the stated conditions, to
> be inscribed on three stone pillars. One is to be set up in the
> marketplace, fixed to the front wall of my house; the second
> should be set up at the entrance of the temple to Caesar, next
> to the city gates; the third at the entrance to the gymnasium,
> so that my philanthropic generosity should be conspicuous
> and acknowledged both by citizens and by visitors to the city . . .
> My idea is that I shall be immortal as a result of this just and
> kindly gift.

CHRISTIAN BURIAL

Over time Christians began to distinguish themselves culturally from certain normal practices. Burial was one. Romans cremated their dead. The Christian apologist Marcus Minucius Felix (*c.* AD 200) explained that early Christians 'did not fear damage to the body from any sort of burial, but kept to the old and better custom of inhumation', because 'all nature points to future resurrection', and he likened the body in the grave to

> trees in winter: they hide their greenness under a deceptive appearance of dryness. What hurry is there anyway to revive and return to life during a hard winter? We must await the springtime of the body.

The underground catacombs, their walls cut with rectangular niches in which the dead were placed, were called *koimêteria* (cf. 'cemetery'), literally, 'sleeping-rooms, dormitories'. The bodies were wrapped in a simple sheet, as Jesus is said to have been, and there they awaited resurrection. A marble slab or clay tiles, marked with the name of the dead and a Christian symbol, hid the body from sight.

Chapter Nine

EPITAPHS AND THE AFTERLIFE

DM

Many epitaphs began with the letters *DM*. These stood for *Dis Manibus*, which meant 'to the Underworld Spirits of the Dead', a multi-purpose collective divinity which the deceased would now be joining. Like all divinities, they survived only as long as humans acknowledged them. That is why there were regular occasions throughout the year when festivals were held in their honour (see p. 150). Only very exceptional Romans actually became fully fledged gods. The first was Julius Caesar, to be followed by emperors and some members of their families. But even so it did not happen automatically. The Senate had to ratify the proposal.

If one did not fancy becoming such a spirit, there were various mystery religions – about which, by definition, we know very little – into which one could be initiated (at a cost). The pay-off was the assurance that one's soul would enjoy benefits of some sort in an afterlife (see p. 174).

JOBS

Epitaphs are a mine of information about all sections of society – free, slave, freedmen, men and women, young and old, great and good, lowly and bad, and even animals, including pigs. A woman called Rhodope buried her dog 'as one would a human'.

Take jobs, for example. Quite apart from political and military roles, we hear of everything from clown to hardwareman, teacher, sacrificial animal slaughterer, butcher, baker and architect to auctioneer, pearl merchant, cattle merchant, doctor and bedchamber slave, clerk, accountant, public slave, stone-sawyer, inn-keeper and buffoon (*scurra*, whence our 'scurrilous'). The clown was memorialized as follows:

> Here is laid the jolly old clown Protogenes, slave of Clulius, who amused very many people with his fooling.

The same merry spirit was evinced by the tomb of the innkeeper Lucius Calidius Eroticus ('Hot Lover') and his wife Fannia Voluptas ('Sexpot'). It is headed

> Lucius Calidius Eroticus made [this monument] for himself and Fannia Voluptas while still alive.

It is followed by a conversation between innkeeper and customer:

Customer: Innkeeper! The bill, please.
Innkeeper: You've had one bottle of wine, and bread. That's one *as*. Sauces, two *asses*.
Customer: Agreed.

Innkeeper: The girl, eight *asses*.

Customer: Agreed as well.

Innkeeper: Hay for the mule, *two asses*.

Customer: That mule – it'll clean me out!

Here is an auctioneer's friendly epitaph (his name is missing):

> Stranger, if you read this name, revile it not ... [name here]
> auctioneer, son of Lucius. This [i.e. tomb] he made in life as an
> everlasting dwelling-place for himself. He believed that what
> nature gave him was a guest-room, and as was proper he enjoyed
> his means in company with his friends. See to it that you, too, so
> use your friends, while you live. Farewell.

Cf. the 'home' theme, p. 166.

THE FIGHTING SCIPIOS

Scipio 'Africanus' was so called because it was he who defeated
Hannibal at Zama (North Africa) in 202 BC. If you wanted a great
and good, this was your man. So the members of his extended family
were keen to be seen to be worthy of one of Rome's most famous
generals. Here is an epitaph to an earlier family member who played
a large part in extending Roman power south into Italy in the third
century BC:

> Lucius Cornelius Scipio Barbatus, Gnaeus' son, a courageous and
> wise man, whose stature perfectly matched his bravery, was aedile,
> consul and censor among you; he took Taurasia and Cisauna in

Samnium; he subdued all Lucania and brought hostages from there.

Observe the emphasis on his political offices and military achievements.

THE CIVILIAN SCIPIOS

This next Scipio held many of the top offices, but his contribution appears to have been less military than legal. After the list comes an *elogium* (a brief hymn of praise). Note the importance of showing that you were worthy of your family line (see p. 147):

> Gnaeus Cornelius Scipio Hispanus, son of Gnaeus, praetor, curule aedile, quaestor, tribune of soldiers (twice); member of the Board of Ten for Judging Lawsuits; member of the Board of Ten for Making Sacrifices. By my good conduct I heaped virtues on the virtues of my clan; I produced a family and sought to equal the exploits of my father. I upheld the praise of my ancestors, so that they are glad that I was created of their line. My honour has ennobled my stock.

This next epitaph probably celebrated a son of Scipio Africanus. The epitaph had to deal with the fact that he died young. It made the best of a bad job:

> For you who wore the distinctive cap of a Flamen Dialis [a priestly office], death cut everything short: honour, fame and virtue, glory and talent. If you had been granted a long life in which to use

these advantages, you would have far surpassed the glory of your ancestors by your achievements. Therefore, Earth gladly takes you in her arms, Scipio – Publius Cornelius, son of Publius.

DEATHS IN THE ORDINARY FAMILY

Such epitaphs create the impression that the Romans were a fairly narrow-minded lot with few interests beyond the military and politics. But the reality of life outside those closed elites gives a rather different picture. Here are some family epitaphs from the less elevated members of society.

A happy marriage
Flavius Agricola seemed a merry sort (cf. p. 154):

Tibur was my home; Flavius Agricola my name. Yes, I'm the one you see reclining here, just as I used to once at dinner, for all the years of life which Fate granted me, taking good care of myself. And I was never short of wine. Flavia Primitiva, my darling wife passed away before me. Chaste worshipper of Isis [see p. 174], attentive to my needs; and graced with every beauty. Thirty happy years we lived together. As a consolation, she left me the fruit of her body, Aurelius Primitivus, to tend my tomb with dutiful affection. Friends who read this: my advice is – mix the wine, tie wreaths round your heads and drink. Don't refuse sex with beautiful girls. After death, earth and ash consume everything else.

A wife on her husband

Here a wife (an ex-slave) remembered her husband:

> Furia Spes, freed by Sempronius Firmus, set up this inscription
> for her beloved husband. We met as boy and girl and from that
> moment on were bound by mutual affection. I lived with him for
> too short a time. Our happiness should have continued, but a cruel
> hand separated us. Sacred Spirits of the Dead, I beg you to protect
> the man I love, whom I have entrusted to you, to be well-disposed
> and kind to him during the hours of night, so that I may see him
> and so that he, too, may be allowed to persuade Fate that I should
> come to him, gently and soon.

Memorials of this sort usually reflected male, not female, priorities.
Not here. This was all about a wife's intimate feelings for her husband.
The usual male concerns about status and achievements were not in
evidence.

Female virtues

The following well-known epitaph adopted a male pattern to
the extent that it identified what a Roman wife *should* be like – all
propriety and hard work in the home:

> Stranger, my message is short. Stand by and read it through. Here
> is the unlovely tomb of a lovely woman. Her parents called her
> Claudia by name. She loved her husband with her whole heart.
> She bore two sons; of these she leaves one on earth; under the
> earth has she placed the other. She was charming in converse, yet

proper in bearing. She kept house, she made wool. That's my last word. Go your way.

The womanly virtue of his wife was similarly noted by this husband:

Here is laid the renowned Sempronia Moschis, dutiful, honourable, chaste and modest, to whom thanks were rendered herewith by her husband for her merits.

So, too, did Lucius the butcher remember his wife:

She who went before me in death, my one and only wife, chaste in body, a loving woman of my heart possessed, lived faithful to her faithful man; in fondness equal to her other virtues, never during bitter times did she shrink from loving duties.

A memorial to Murdia, mostly about the detail of the dispensations in her will, summed up the virtues traditionally attached to the Good Woman:

My dearest mother deserved greater praise than all others, since in modesty, propriety, chastity, obedience, wool-working, industry and loyalty she was on an equal level with other good women, nor did she take second place to any woman in virtue, work and wisdom in times of danger.

Here a male doctor praised his wife for medical skill equal to his own, in terms quite unexceptional in the ancient (if not the modern) world:

Farewell, my wife, Pantheia, from your husband, whose grief at your devastating death is inconsolable. Hera the goddess of marriage has never before beheld such a wife, excelling in beauty, wisdom and discretion. All the children you bore resemble me, and you took care of your husband and your children. You kept the tiller of our domestic life on a straight course, and you exalted our shared reputation as doctors. Nor, even though you are a woman, did you fall short of me in skill. Therefore, Glycon your husband built for you this tomb, which also covers the body of our immortal Philadelphus, and in which I myself shall also lie.

STORIES BEHIND EPITAPHS

Many epitaphs explained the dramatic circumstances in which people died – crushed by a crowd, killed in battle or at sea, killed by falling roof tiles, deceived by a bull, and so on. Others were briefer, but still had a story to tell.

Regina

To the spirits of the departed: Regina, freedwoman and wife – Barates from Palmyra - from the Catuvellaunian tribe - of years XXX.

This epitaph accompanied a sculpture of a well-dressed woman, with necklace and bracelets, spinning equipment (always a mark of the faithful, hard-working wife) and jewellery box (with lock). *Regina* meant 'Queen'. But she was no queen in the technical sense, because the second word is *liberta*, 'freedwoman': she was 'Queenie'. The inscription tells us that she originated from the Catuvellauni, a tribe that lived around St Albans. So down south she was probably sold into slavery –perhaps to raise money for her poverty-stricken family – and taken up north to South Shields.

Her husband was *Barates Palmyrenus* – Barates from Palmyra in Syria! What was Barates doing in South Shields, over 4,000 miles from home? There is evidence that he was doing business with the Roman army, in the international economic world of the Roman Empire, perhaps as a standard-maker. He fell in love with the slave he had bought, freed her and married her.

Queenie died aged thirty. It does not say how. There is a further inscription *below* the Latin – in Palmyrene. This says: 'Regina, freedwoman of Barates, alas.' Roman epitaphs tended to be stiff, formal productions. Only in his native language could Barates express his feelings.

From slave to free

Slaves could not legitimately marry, but they could still have children. This monument recorded the legitimate marriage of *former* slaves, who had been given their freedom by their owner Lucius. It was probably put up by her husband Aurelius:

> Aurelius Hermia, freedman of Lucius, a butcher by trade from the Viminal Hill. My partner who departed this life before me was pure of body and loving of spirit. She was the only one for me, and lived her life faithful to her faithful husband, with equal devotion. She

never failed in her duties through self-interest or greed: Aurelia, freedwoman of Lucius.

Aurelia Philematio, freedwoman of Lucius. In life, I was given the name Aurelia Philematium ('little kiss') and led a chaste, modest and sheltered life, faithful to my husband. Aurelius, my husband, whom I now sadly miss, was a fellow freedman. He was, in fact, much more to me than even a parent. He took me into his care at the age of seven. Now at the age of forty, I fall into the hands of death. He flourished in the eyes of others because of my constant and close support.

A cheated gladiator?

This next epitaph commemorated the gladiator Diodorus:

After breaking my opponent Demetrius I did not kill him immediately.
Fate and the cunning treachery of the referee [?] killed me.

The suggested storyline behind this epitaph is as follows: Diodorus had Demetrius at his mercy, and was expecting the crowd to give its verdict. But the referee, deciding that Demetrius was not down and out, allowed him to continue fighting and the result was that it was Diodorus who was killed. Clearly those who put up the epitaph felt there was some dirty work going on here.

Unhappy accidents

Here was someone killed, apparently, because of a curse (see Appendix):

Bound by curse-spells over a long period, she now lies here,

Her life ripped out of her by force to be returned to nature.
Her Spirit of Death and the sky gods will take revenge for this
crime.

Here an accident at play was responsible:

A dummy weapon was rashly thrown without intention to kill but
Hit me and buried itself in the top of my head.

This hero paid the price for his rashness:

DM: and the eternal memory of Lucius Secundus Octavius from
Trier. He met a most bitter end: escaping semi-naked from a fire he
had no thought for his own safety but tried to rescue something
from the flames. A wall collapsed and fell on him, returning his
communal spirit to nature and his body to its origins.

Winners

Some epitaphs went into great detail, especially if one had been
successful, perhaps against the odds, as was this Numidian peasant:

I was born of poor parents; my father had neither an income
nor his own house. From the day of my birth I always cultivated
our fields; neither my land nor I ever had any rest . . . I left my
neighbourhood for twelve years and reaped the harvest for
another man, under a fiery sun; for eleven years I was then chief
of the harvest gang, gathering the corn in the fields of Numidia.
Thanks to my labours, and being content with very little, I finally
became master of a house and a property: today I live at ease. I

have even achieved honours: I was called on to sit in the Senate of my city, and, though once a hayseed [rusticulus], I became censor. I have watched my children and grandchildren grow up around me; my life has been occupied, peaceful and honoured by all.

This soldier rather fancied his own achievements:

I am that man who was once famous about the Pannonian shores [a province south of the Danube], foremost among a thousand strong men from Batavia [a Germanic tribe]. With the Emperor for judge, I was able to swim the vast surface of the deep Danube fully armed. I have shot an arrow and, while it hung in the air before descending to earth, split it with a second shaft. No Roman or barbarian soldier could beat me with the javelin, no Persian with the bow. I lie here with this stone to keep the record of my deeds. It will see whether anyone else after me can duplicate my feats; but I am my own example, for I was the first to do these things.

Losers?

Other epitaphs had something of an edge to them:

While life was granted, he lived a miser,
Sparing of his fortune, envious even of himself.
He ordered that, after his death, a master-craftsman
creatively sculpt him, reclining convivially here.

In this one, the composer of the epitaph (presumably the father) covered his own back against accusations of tricky dealing (on adoption, see footnote p. 52):

Here lies Vitalis, first the slave, then the son of Gaius Lavius Faustus.
I was born in his home as a slave. I lived sixteen years and I was
a salesman in a shop. I was pleasant and well liked, but I was
snatched away by the gods. I beg you, travellers and passers-by, if
ever I shortchanged you to bring more profit to my father, please
forgive me. And I beg you, by the gods above and below, that you
treat my father and mother with kindness and respect. Farewell.

SOME THEMES IN EPITAPHS

The poet Ovid retold the myth of the great singer Orpheus going
down to the Underworld to try to bring his beloved Eurydice back
to life on earth. He hoped to achieve this by using his power of song
to enchant the fierce gatekeepers of the Underworld into submission.
Here is part of the song that Ovid put in his mouth:

> In everything we're **owed to you**. We linger here brief space,
> And soon or late we **find our way** to your **one resting-place**.
> **We all are bound** for there, that place **our final home**; while your
> Long empire ruling human kind continues, ever more.

The bold passages reflected typical themes that could be found across
epitaphs: death as a debt repaid; as a journey; as inescapable; and as
a final home.

Here are some examples of these themes, followed by others.
Please note that → indicates either a one-line extract from an epitaph
or the first line of a longer extract.

Debt

The idea that life was a loan and therefore one owed a debt to death was one such theme. Among epitaphs one finds lines such as:

→ Since you ask, an unjust creditor has recalled the debt before its due date.

→ What nature gave, nature recalled.

Journey

That life was a road or a journey towards death was another common metaphor, though relatively rare in epitaphs:

→ One road is common to all mankind.

→ My journey lasted 25 years.

Homes and inns

Resting places, homes and inns were frequently deployed, often to contrast a temporary accommodation on earth with the eternal resting place in the tomb or in the Underworld:

→ This home (i.e. tomb) is eternal, here am I laid, here I shall be for ever.

Since home meant so much to Romans, the tomb could make a good substitute:

→ Here is our home, here we shall live together.

In that light, it could be a consoling thought:

→ This is my eternal home, this is my rest from labour, my posterity.

The tomb could also be an inn:

> → The friendly Earth provides an inn for bones.

> → 'This is your inn.' 'I come unwillingly. But come I must.'

But it was sometimes life that was the inn:

> The rich man builds a home, the wise man a monument;
> The former is the inn for body, the latter its home.

This epitaph made a good joke about the image:

> All a person needs. Bones reposing sweetly, I am not anxious about
> suddenly being short of food. I do not suffer from arthritis, and I
> am not indebted because of being behind in my rent. In fact, my
> lodgings are permanent – and free!

Inevitability

There was some degree of consolation in the thought that everyone eventually went this way:

> → All we mortals are held in the grip of the same fate.
> → We all share the same home, which no man can escape.
> → Traveller! As you, so I [was]; as I, so everyone.

The above by no means exhausted the number of motifs commonly to be found in epitaphs. Here are some more.

Contrast

Most moving of all were those epitaphs that compared and contrasted the exuberance of life with the blankness of death:

→ I who lived twenty years, fresh-cheeked, in the flower of youth,
was a soldier; now from a soldier I am become dust.

→ My loyal wife, dear Sabina, lies under this stone.
She alone was more skilled than her husband;
Her voice was delightful, she played the lyre;
But suddenly taken, she falls silent.

Gods, death, Fate and Fortune

Assorted external agencies were regularly credited with causing
death when it was not clear why the person had died:

→ Death suddenly snatched him away.

→ Envious Pluto [god of the Underworld] snatched him away.

→ Fortune, which controls the unpredictable fates of men . . .

→ A stone covers my bones. That's good. Fortune, farewell.

→ Fortune, are you pleased with this grave?

→ When Fate calls, none can resist.

→ Envious Fate made all our prayers in vain.

→ I lived as I wanted. Why I am dead, I have no idea.

Two feelings were at work here: first, that death was as often as
not a complete mystery, leaving you helpless in the grip of some
inexplicable, generalized power; second, that such powers were
malign, out to get you, unless you could somehow unlock the secret
of keeping them onside.

In this light, some epitaphs avoided the mental torment created by
this way of thinking and expressed the idea that death was welcome
(cf. p. 167):

→ I have escaped the disorders of illness and the great evils of life;
Now I am free of punishment and enjoy peace and quiet.

A charioteer, without expressing a wish to die, put it this way:

→ I smashed into the corner of the turning post – a desirable way
to die:
I died as I prayed I would, though it was a serious accident.

Consoling the bereaved

Another common motif was a personal appeal by the deceased not to
grieve for him or her:

→ Don't grieve, dear friend, at my lot:
Age hurried on, Fate supplied my end.

→ Why lament my loss? Fate's order is not upset.
Human affairs are like apples:
Either they fall in due season or are picked too soon.

Or one could argue that at least the deceased had been given a
proper burial:

→A faithful friend set up this monument for you:
I have carried out the final duty I owed.

This most eloquent memorial began traditionally, and was then
put into the mouth of the deceased herself, Agileia Prima, consoling
her husband (from 'At the time . . . '):

→ Wife beyond eternity; most chaste and modest and frugal,
who loved her husband and his house and all his possessions

innocently. Quintus Oppius Secundus, her husband, made
this for the deserving one and for himself. At the time I was
begotten, nature granted me twice ten years, upon the
fulfillment of which, on the seventh day thereafter, freed of the
laws [that bind one to life] I was given over to unending rest.
This life was given to me, [so] Oppius, do not fear Lethe [a river
in the Underworld], for it is foolish to lose joy of life while fearing
death at all times. For death is the nature, not the punishment of
mankind; whoever happens to be born, therefore also confronts
death. Master Oppius, husband, do not lament me because I
have preceded you. I await your arrival in the eternal marriage
bed. Be well, my survivors, and all other men and women, be
well.

Attracting sympathy

Because the dead were buried outside the city, roads were lined
with tombstones and therefore attracted the attention of passers-by.
Epitaphs often urged them to pay attention, or expressed thanks for
their doing so. It was a way of engaging their sympathy and perhaps
encouraging people to remember them:

→ If mud or dust is perhaps slowing you down, traveller,
   Or heat and thirst are holding you up, read this.

→ Guest, it's gratifying of you to halt at this resting place:
   May you be successful and healthy, and sleep without a care.

→ What anyone of you would wish for me in death,
   May that turn out to be the case for you, in life and death.

Sometimes the passer-by was invited to shed tears:

→ You who will die, do not deny tears when you read this.

There was also some consolation if two lovers were buried together:

→ Happy couple! If there is glory in death, this is it:
The grave joins you together, as did the bed.

POETS ON LOVE AND DEATH

The passionate poet, desperate to make love to his girl, regularly argued that their relationship was unique – personal, private, quite unlike anything that anyone had ever experienced; and then again that, since death was all around them, she had better make the most of it while she was still young and desirable. As the Roman poet Catullus said, 'Once our brief light has set, there is nothing but a night of perpetual sleep' (i.e. rather than of making love).

Building on such themes, ancient poets liked to imagine what their own funeral would be like and how their current loved one would react to it. The poet might reject the idea of a normal funeral with its processions and trumpets, where family, friends and relations would gather (see p. 143ff) in favour of a private, poor man's ceremony, with just the loved one there, praying the earth lie gently on him; in death his shade would still love her; all his tomb would say was that he loved one woman alone; and so on.

The poet Propertius, having been summoned by his girl, imagined being murdered on his way to her. If so, she would bring perfumes and wreaths and guard the grave. But he begged her not to bury him along the roadside, trampled by the ghastly mob who treated graves with disdain (p. 48). No, she must bury him in a secluded spot, shaded by trees or in sand dunes, well away from the rabble: 'It will bring me no pleasure to have my name on display by a road.'

Even in death, the poet fantasized, his love would still be secret and his obsequies (uniquely) tended by one single person. So his funeral would be equally unique, with none of the traditional fanfares.

DEATH: THE END OR A TRANSITION?

Death as the end

On matters of the afterlife, our world nods to 'authoritative' texts such as the Bible. As a result, ancient flexible and open-ended beliefs and practices on such matters may strike us as odd: it seems that your beliefs were up to you.

Lucretius (first century BC), a philosopher from the school of Epicurus, had no doubts about the matter: the world, men and gods were all made of atoms; and gods had little interest is us, alive or dead. To clinch it, he came up with twenty-nine proofs of the *mortality* of the soul. So from atoms we came and to atoms we returned, and that was that. He argued with almost religious fervour that men were too influenced by the living body to realize that

> in the reality of death there will be no other self that could exist
> to lament that he had been deprived of life and could stand there
> and grieve at being lacerated or burnt.

After all, Lucretius went on, if people believed that after death they would be eaten by wild beasts, why were they so relaxed about being cremated or laid out on a slab of cold marble or buried under a weight of earth?

The elite had little time for popular belief in ghosts of the dead haunting the earth or an afterlife of suffering. Cicero said that those who believed 'the deceased were still alive' either had no grasp of causation or were influenced by apparitions; those who believed that the deceased had been deprived of the comforts of life were equally irrational, as were those who thought souls could suffer in the Underworld. Cicero could also joke about the ritual involved: 'It is foolish to tear one's hair in grief: grief is rarely diminished by baldness.' Cato the Elder (according to Cicero, p. 132) and Socrates (p. 99) offered a hopeful, agnostic view of the matter.

Seneca concluded that we should try to die as happily as we tried to live, and that meant dying gladly, i.e. not pointlessly fighting the inevitable, for that would merely make the experience miserable: 'there is only one chain that binds us to life, and that is the love of life'.

Death as an afterlife

In Homer, the soul (*psukhê*) was not a living entity, but simply an insubstantial image of the dead person (see below). An actual after*life* which the *psukhê* could actively enjoy seems to have been associated first with the cult of Orpheus, to be adopted by philosophers like Pythagoras (sixth century BC). He believed the *psukhê* did not die, but was reincarnated into humans or animals (hence he advocated strict vegetarianism). The Egyptian goddess Isis had a following in the Greek and Roman worlds, as a sort of Demeter mother-goddess, associated also with the moon. Her worshippers were promised a more enjoyable afterlife. Mithras, an Indo-Iranian god, became popular in the Empire: for Romans he was primarily a sun god. This mystery religion (Greek *mustêria*, 'secret rites') may have offered the *psukhê* of the initiate an ascent to heaven after death.

The view from epitaphs

To judge from epitaphs, common opinion was mixed. Here someone of philosophical bent was celebrated as follows:

> → While I lived I taught what life and death was;
> As a result I understand the eternal joys of the soul.

Here the deceased hoped to meet up with a loved one again:

> → And there will be the consolation that I shall eventually see you
> And when I am dead, I shall be joined as a shade to your image.

By contrast, a very common refrain in epitaphs expressed a doubt about the possibility of life after death:

> → If there are Spirits of the Dead, may the earth lie light upon you.

This sentiment appeared in many forms:

> → Whoever you are, lucky traveller, may it not be difficult
> For you to say 'If the Spirits of the Dead know anything after death,
> Let the bones of Antonius and Proculus lie softly.'

And then there were those epitaphs that expressed no hope of immortality at all:

→ Live for the days and hours: there is nothing else.

The death of Pompeia was similarly remembered. Note the emphasis on the randomness of Fortune, which seemed to offer so much:

→ Here lie the bones of Pompeia, eldest daughter.
  Fortune pledges things to many,
  Guarantees them not to any.
  Live for each day, live for the hours,
  Since nothing is for always yours.

The following lines appeal to anyone reading the epitaph:

→ We are nothing. We were mortal. Look back, reader,
  How quickly we recede into nothing from nothing.

More convivially (see p. 157):

→ Friends who read this: my advice is - mix the wine,
  Tie wreaths round your heads and drink.
  Don't refuse sex with beautiful girls.
  After death, earth and ash consume everything else.

This one put it very simply:

→ I was not, I was, I am not, I care not.

Popular sentiments

Sayings and proverbs sang a less hopeful song. Observations such as 'It is not death, but the approach to death, that is bitter' and 'We men die nowhere better than when we have lived happily' were rare.

More common were the gloomy assertions: 'Life is short except in evils'; 'Death is good for a man when it ends the evils of life'. It all added up to: life is hazardous and disagreeable, but it is all we have, so make the most of it. This one tells its own tale:

> Baths, drink and sex corrupt our flesh and blood.
> Baths, drink and sex, still, make life very good.

Views of old age were equally gloomy: it was irrelevant, serving no purpose, foolish and unaccountable. That being the case, why bother to be good? Wisdom in the old was reckoned to be a quality attached only to the elite.

The Christian epitaph

The Christian promise of a guaranteed afterlife changed the whole basis on which the pagan world thought about death, including its epitaphs. But one could still find in some the basic *reflexes* of the traditional 'pagan' form:

→ Do not shed tears at the death of your husband,
Do not lament such a one to whom eternal life is given in exchange for death.

→ Petronius, you gave my body to the earth, but my soul to Christ.

→ I ask in the name of the Lord of All and Jesus of Nazareth that
you do not touch me nor violate my grave, for you will plead
your cause against me before the tribunal of the eternal judge.

In the following epitaph, the pagan world view is specifically
denied:

→ If mental power and a more confident experience of the Light
returns to one who died in Christ, he does not encounter
Tartarus or the Cimmerian lake.

But here, Paradise had a distinctly classical feel:

→ No gloomy Erebus, no pale image of death, but a secure peace
surrounds you and playful dances among the happy souls and
pleasant places of the righteous.

Many more examples of pagan influence could be adduced: even
the *Manes* turned up from time to time! Over time, inevitably, these
faded away.

IMAGES OF THE UNDERWORLD

In the absence of a holy book, Greeks and Romans provide us with as
many images of the Underworld as there were Greeks and Romans. It
could be located underground or at the far end of the world. It could
be a place of punishment, bliss or something in between: mystery
religions did indeed offer 'bliss' to initiates, and a number of thinkers
expressed the view that really heinous crimes would be punished after
death.

Odysseus among the dead

Homer's *Odyssey* (*c*. 700 BC) contained the first Western version of the Underworld. Odysseus wanted to consult the dead prophet Teiresias. Far from going down to the Underworld, he travelled to the distant entrance to it, where he sacrificed animals and filled a ditch with their blood. The ghosts of the dead rose up to drink it: only then could they actually speak.

First Odysseus chatted with an old comrade, then Teiresias, and finally his mother. Then the goddess of the Underworld decided that Odysseus should (for some unstated reason) hear the stories or observe a swarm of dead heroines, twelve named and assorted others. This episode finished, the goddess duly drove them off and Odysseus resumed talking with comrades from the Trojan War, including Achilles (see below).

Then without warning a crowd of mythical heroes appeared who did not need to drink the blood. Three were suffering punishment, and last of all came Heracles. From Odysseus' description of these encounters, it looks as if he was suddenly actually *in* the Underworld.

This is all a bit of a pig's ear, a mishmash of necromancy (calling up the dead) and Underworld travel adventure. But apart from the final scene, there is no indication that the Underworld was a place of punishment or of eternal bliss. It was a place, as Odysseus' mother told him, 'where the soul slips away like a dream [from the funeral pyre] and goes fluttering on its ways'.

Odysseus and the ghost of Achilles

Achilles, in the company of his beloved companion-in-arms Patroclus, expressed amazement that Odysseus 'dare come below to Hades' realm [i.e. the Underworld, which he had not, but never mind] where the dead live on as mindless, disembodied ghosts'. Odysseus explained that he had come to consult Teiresias and urged Achilles, who surely 'ruled among the dead', not to grieve at his fate. Achilles was having none of this:

> Do not gloss over death to *me*, illustrious Odysseus. I would rather work the soil as a serf on hire to some landless, impoverished peasant than be king of all these lifeless dead. Come, give me news of that fine son of mine. Did he follow me to the war to play a leading part or not?

That was what Achilles, the Greeks' greatest hero-warrior, made of death – he would rather be a serf, a nobody, but *alive*, with at least a chance of doing great things, than live out that grey, unmotivated existence. When Odysseus told him that his son Neoptolemus had performed magnificently:

> So I spoke, and the soul of swift-footed Achilles departed, taking great strides across the asphodel field, thrilled that I had given him news of his son's renown.

What a moment: though neutered by Hades, Achilles could still rise to the news of his son's heroism in war – a true son of his father. That was the life, that was the only life!

So much for Homer's picture of the Underworld.

Aeneas in the Underworld

In his *Aeneid* – an epic about the Trojan hero Aeneas, the mythical founder of the Roman race – the poet Virgil (70–19 bc) presented an entirely different picture of the Underworld. Aeneas wanted to consult his dead father Anchises. He was led down to Hades by a Sibyl, a woman with prophetic powers, as his guide. This is how this section began:

> They walked in the darkness of that lonely night with shadows all about them, through the empty halls of Dis and his desolate kingdom, as men walk in a wood by the sinister light of a fitful moon when Jupiter has buried the sky in shade and black night has robbed all things of their colour.
>
> Before the entrance hall of Orcus, in the very throat of hell, Grief and Revenge have made their beds and Old Age lives there in despair, with white-faced Disease and Fear and Hunger, corrupter of men, and squalid Poverty, things dreadful to look upon, and Death and Drudgery besides. Then there are Sleep, Death's sister, perverted Pleasures, murderous War astride the threshold, the iron chambers of the Furies and raving Discord with blood-soaked ribbons binding her viperous hair.
>
> In the middle, a huge dark elm spreads out its ancient arms, the resting-place, so they say, of flocks of idle dreams, one clinging under every leaf. Here, too, are all manner of monstrous beasts, Centaurs stabling inside the gate, Scyllas – half-dogs, half-women – Briareus with his hundred heads, the Hydra of Lerna hissing fiercely, the Chimaera armed in fire, Gorgons and Harpies and the triple phantom of Geryon.

Now Aeneas drew his sword in sudden alarm to meet them
with naked steel as they came at him, and if his wise companion
had not warned him that this was the fluttering of disembodied
spirits, a mere semblance of living substance, he would have
rushed upon them and parted empty shadows with steel.
(tr. David West)

Crossing the river

Aeneas and the Sibyl reached the river Acheron and met the ferryman
Charon. Crowds of the dead swarmed along that side of the river,
unable to cross, because (as the Sibyl explained) they were unburied.
Aeneas and the Sibyl crossed, passed the three-headed dog Cerberus
(the Sibyl drugged it), met another crowd of the dead being judged
by King Minos, and various other unhappy souls. They passed the
place of punishment, and eventually reached the homes of the blessed,
where they met Anchises. When Anchises had 'foreseen' the whole
history of the Roman race (up until 19 BC, at any rate), Aeneas and
the Sibyl returned to the upper world via the gates of ivory, through
which 'false dreams ascend to the upper world'.

And that was Virgil's picture of the Underworld, serving *his*
purposes.

Er ... Plato

At the heart of Plato's *Republic* was a discussion led by Socrates about
what an ideal state should look like. The central argument was that
such a state could come about only if everyone had a clear vision of
the difference between right and wrong. The dialogue ended with a
myth about a soldier called Er, who miraculously returned from the

dead and described what happened in the afterlife. It transpired that the souls' choice of their *next* life was the key issue.

First, lots were randomly scattered among the souls to determine the order in which they selected their next existence. Then the future lives (human and animal) were placed in front of them. There being more lives than souls, even the last to choose had a good pick. 'The first to choose should take care,' says Hades' intermediary, 'and the last need not despair.' At this point, Plato interjected:

> This is clearly an absolutely critical moment for a person – which is why during this life we must do everything to find someone who can tell us how to distinguish good lives from bad.

Soul choice

Er then went on to describe how the first soul unhesitatingly chose the most powerful tyranny he could – not noticing it contained the fate of eating his own children and other terrible crimes. Orpheus chose to become a swan, Agamemnon an eagle, Ajax a lion, and Odysseus, tired of hardship, a humble private citizen.

They made their choices, however, with these words of Lady Lachesis, the daughter of Necessity, ringing in their ears:

> Goodness makes its own rules. Each of you will be good to the extent that you value it. Responsibility lies with the chooser, not with the god.

And that was Plato's myth of the Underworld, designed to suit his purposes.

Things do not change. We still *know* no more about any afterlife than the ancients did, and never will, and consequently have no option but to make it up. On this matter, there are many different opinions, depending on religious beliefs, or none.

Gods, death and life

Pagan gods, being immortal, steered well clear of the dead and played no part in the transition from life to death: Hades, the god of the Underworld, ruled there and other gods stayed well away. Further, Hades – he had no name other than the place – was not a god of moral purity or such-like. He had virtually no cult: he just wanted the place kept nice and full of the dead.

But there was another, sunnier version of Hades, called Pluto. He had a wife called Persephone or Proserpina (the same, only different; think, for example, Father Christmas/Santa Claus). Pluto's name derived from the Greek *ploutos*, 'wealth' (cf. 'plutocracy'), because the earth was full of minerals and provided seeds for the harvest.

As we have seen, the ancients did not agonize about the afterlife: the Underworld was not generally seen as a place of punishment or reward, where a reckoning had to be faced. This had one important consequence. Ancient religion has been called performance-indexed piety: it was all about carrying out the right rituals at the right time. Do that and you would probably be OK. So in the absence of any expectations of an afterlife, what counted was success and failure in *this* life, and success depended on having the gods on your side. Consequently, if one dishonoured the gods by, for example, refusing to acknowledge them, one would not have to wait until the afterlife for punishment – it would be visited on you in the here and now.

AVOIDING THE DROP

Could a man somehow cheat death? Ancient myth played with the idea. The Babylonian hero Gilgamesh went down to the Underworld to seek immortality, while the goddess Calypso offered immortality to Odysseus if he would stay with her and not return from the Trojan War to his wife Penelope. The goddess Thetis tried to save her son Achilles from death by dipping him in the river Styx – forgetting to include his eventually fatal heel – and the famous singer Orpheus charmed his way down to Hades in an attempt to bring back his beloved Eurydice.

The point is that all these efforts failed. Greeks had no illusions about the matter. For them, there was one chasm that could not be bridged and that was the chasm separating mortals from immortals. The ultimate *hubris* was to attempt it – a sure way to guarantee the fate that you were trying to avoid. The myth of Eous (the goddess Dawn) and her mortal lover Tithonus demonstrated that even the gods got it wrong: Eous gave him eternal life, but forgot at the same time to give him eternal youth.

Chapter Ten: Epilogue

MEMENTO MORI

Roman ideas about how to deal with ageing are parroted by our media almost every day: eat sensibly, enjoy company, and keep mind and body alert and active. But death itself is a different matter. It is an emotional business, for the living and the dying; and to that extent the *intellectual* arguments that the ancients and others use to deal with it can ring hollow (cf. Seneca p. 89); as do fatuous assertions that one 'will fight this thing' or proclamations of your own heroism in facing it bravely. Herein lies the main difference between today's world and the Romans. Romans never imagined they could 'fight' death. They dealt with it by facing the hard facts of the real world. Modern man tries to escape them.

Today Western man lives in a fast-changing world in which, thanks to science and technology, the natural world can be judged no longer good enough and therefore must be manipulated to meet his every whim. Every day one hears someone saying, 'We must find a cure for ageing', as if ageing were an illness or represented some sort of correctable failure in the evolutionary process. The inevitable UN spokesman recently intoned that one of the great challenges the world faced was 'the future of ageing'. What he should have said, but dared not, was 'the future of dying'.

The economic world is equally manoeverable. Thanks to technology and a range of financial mechanisms, industry and business must now combine to ensure growth and ever-increasing material prosperity for all. Indeed, this seems to be one of the main purposes, almost an inherent duty, of government.

The possibilities offered by this brave new world now at man's beck and call seem limitless.

But then modern man comes up against death, and finds it very hard to believe that an unconditional point of no return should be allowed to remain in an environment which seems so adaptable to his will. Something must be done about it, and many are convinced that something *can* be done about it. In the meantime, at least, one must be given the means to resist the ageing process – or even reverse it – as if there were some compelling moral imperative in, or innate human virtue or benefit to, living longer and longer.

One response is for man to strive to maintain an image of vigorous youth, hoping his sixty will be the new twenty. The Latin *imago* meant 'representation, reflection in a mirror, hallucination, semblance, copy, appearance, death mask'. So as Seneca put it: 'Are you lengthening your life – or your death?' It is to assume that somehow the ultimate goal, the quintessential expression, of everything that it is to be human is to be so physically engineered throughout later life to look as if you are not who you are. The alternative – looking or acting or even enjoying your age – seems unbearable. This makes dying even more unfair, since as a result of modern medicine we might be feeling like a teenager only to be told by the doctor that in fact the Grim Reaper was about to inconvenience us terminally.

For the Romans, the one world they had was that of Nature – animals, air, water, earth, sand, clay, some metals, rocks, woods, other vegetation and, of course, men (Romans did not distinguish between humans and nature as we do). All was in its raw state, except in so far as fire could change it (for example, cooking, metalwork, pottery) or man experiment with it in limited ways (for example, papyrus, concrete, the arch – all important developments). The only power sources were wind, wave, man and beast. And that was it: *nothing synthetic at all.* Only after the Industrial Revolution, beginning in the eighteenth century, when for the first time heat was turned into work (via steam) on a significant scale and man started to devise many different ways of capturing and exploiting energy (of which electricity is perhaps the most stunning fruit) did our modern world become possible.

Further, the Roman world was controlled by the seasons, and these were at the mercy of the elements, which determined whether you could grow anything and therefore eat and live. A bad drought and thousands died. Useful animals such as sheep and goats were at the mercy of predators and disease.

So too was man, the predators including other men. The bottom line was the fight for survival, for which killing men was a duty. No life was held sacred. A people that could not defend itself against an invading army did not survive, or only as slaves. It was the survival of the fittest, and you had better make sure that was you. That was Nature for you, the way the world *was.* There was nothing that could be done about it.

At the same time, that desire to compete so that one always came out on top – in war as in politics – was accompanied by an acknowledgement that there were alternatives: cooperation, for example, live and let live. After all, it was not as if Romans did not have perfectly good words for pity, sympathy, mercy, forgiveness and so on. But there was nothing absolute, in a Christian sense, about those values: what was really at stake in, for example, the question 'Do I kill or forgive?' was hard-headed utility. Practical people, the Romans.

Such were the unchanging conditions of existence for a Roman, which he acknowledged in his worship of the gods – for the state of the natural world was *their* doing. The main feature of that world, and crucial to its survival, was the eternal pattern, divinely controlled, of *changing* seasons, exemplified in the story of Demeter. When her daughter Persephone was seized by Pluto, god of the Underworld (p. 163), all living things began to die. The problem was resolved when Persephone returned for six months to earth, when fruitfulness returned, followed by the six barren months of winter. Worship of the gods was for the most part tied into that pattern, to ensure that the six fruitful months did not fail. Nothing that man could do would guarantee that.

The pattern of the seasonal life and death of Nature was repeated in the life and death of men. That does not imply that, when a Roman confronted his own death, he was thrilled at the prospect. That is clear from the way in which thinkers like Seneca and Lucretius assured him there was nothing to be worried about. But he had no expectation of being able to do anything about it, let alone feel personally offended by it. It was the way the natural world *was*. The idea that he might 'fight' it would have appeared too absurd for words, like asking (as Seneca did): should you obey Nature or Nature obey you? The contrast with the modern world's reaction to this question is clear: Nature should obey us, and since we do not like the idea of ageing or death, it is our right that both should be off the menu. Yet what a paradox this is, at a time when man's ignoring of the limits to which the natural world can be pushed (global warming being the main example) has become such a major ethical issue.

The ancients' more realistic view did not make the end of life any easier to bear. A chorus in a play by Sophocles sang:

> Best not to be born at all but, if you are,
> To return whence you came as soon as possible

and went on to describe old age as

> unregarded, powerless, unsociable, unfriended,
> where misery couples with misery.

That vein of pessimism permeated all ancient life and thought, and it is not surprising. Life was short and brutal and the body, young or old, was at the mercy of every passing virus and bacterium. Man had no option but to accept what Nature or events (otherwise known as 'Fate') threw at him, with as much stoical good grace as possible. Neither man nor the state could do anything about any of them.

Given, then, that you could not fight it, you had to accept it. In that respect, the Romans thought rather as Ecclesiastes ('the preacher') did in the Old Testament, that 'all is vanity' (i.e. futile) and one makes the best of what is on offer when one can:

¹To every thing there is a season, and a time to every purpose under the heaven:

²A time to be born, and a time to die; a time to plant, and a time to pluck up that which is planted;

³A time to kill, and a time to heal; a time to break down, and a time to build up;

⁴A time to weep, and a time to laugh; a time to mourn, and a time to dance.

This was the world as the Romans understood it: eternal, unchanging and unchangeable, of polar extremes but in complete accord with Nature, with a time for everything, including dying.

The contrast with the modern belief that nature is there as a challenge to our abilities to alter – and so improve – it could not be sharper. One way, for example, in which nature is challenged every hour of the day is through visual media. Many will remember a woman exclaiming 'What a beautiful baby!' and the mother replying, 'Yes, but you should see the photographs.' When the Queen recently appeared in a programme talking about her coronation in 1953, it was a pleasant surprise to see that it actually *was* the Queen and not some passing Gwyneth or Meryl, who would surely have been far more convincing. As for 'virtual reality', consider the meaning of the word 'virtual': synonyms would include 'almost', 'quasi', 'nearly', 'fairly'. In other words, not reality at all, but simply another image, picture, representation brought into the comfort of your very own living room. That 'virtual' is, of course, a brilliant choice of words on the part of those offering simple delusion. It sounds so wholesome, so *virtuous*, so much more real than reality, an illusion that the delusion-peddlers do all they can to promote.

Romans did not enjoy the immeasurable privilege of becoming their own fantasy at the flick of a switch. They had a clearer vision of what could and could not be expected from real – as opposed to reel – life. One tactic was to seek an immortal reputation, so that one lived for ever on the lips of men. Another was to argue for the immortality of the soul. Far more practical was to make the most of what life had to offer.

Ausonius (*c.* AD 309–92) provided an example. He was a Roman living in what is now Bordeaux. A teacher, public servant and poet, he is the source of the name Château Ausone, home of the famous wine. He was also a poet, hymning, for example, the glories of the river Moselle. In the following poem, he pinpointed one of the very great pleasures – all things being equal that old age had waiting for us. The last four lines are a (very) abbreviated paraphrase:

My dearest wife, no change for us:
Let's always keep those names
We called each other on that night
Of our first nuptial games;
So that for us, in oldest age,
It never fails to be
That I am still your 'Oo! Young *man!*'
And you're 'My girl!' to me.
How old we are
Will matter not one jot:
We'll have life's richness,
And the years forgot.

The great Wendy Cope put it in a simpler, more modern vernacular:

> If we were never going to die, I might
> Not hug you quite as often, or as tight.

And then, having made the most of life, one could acknowledge what a relief death was. We have already seen Cicero thinking of death in old age in terms of a fruit reaching its ripeness and falling naturally from the tree, and of a man reaching land after a long voyage. The Stoic emperor Marcus Aurelius put it this way:

> How trivial life is: yesterday a drop of semen, today a mummy or ashes. Spend therefore these fleeting moments as Nature would have you spend them, and then go to your rest with a good grace, as an olive falls in season, with a blessing for the earth that bore it and a thanksgiving to the tree that gave it life.

Appendix

A CURSE TABLET

A curse tablet was usually made of lead. The curse was inscribed on it and normally placed in a grave or well. It urged the spirits of the early dead, who roamed the earth until the 'right' time for their death came, to beg the gods of the dead to carry out the wishes of the curser. About 1,500 curse tablets have been found from around the Mediterranean, and about 130 from a spring under the baths in Bath, England.

The tablet often had a nail driven through it. Hence its name, *defixio*, literally 'a nailing down', referring to the person who was the subject of the curse, in this case one Plotius. As will become apparent, this tablet was written by someone on whom Plotius himself had placed a curse. Translated from the Latin, it is dated to about 50 BC. For Proserpina and Pluto, see p. 183:

> Good and beautiful Proserpina, wife of Pluto, or Salvia, if you prefer that I call you so, snatch away the health, the body, the complexion, the strength, and the faculties of Plotius.

Hand him over to Pluto, your husband. May he not be able to escape this [curse] by his wits. Hand him over to fevers – four-day, three-day and daily fevers – so that they wrestle and struggle with him. Let them overcome him to the point where they snatch away his soul.

Thus I give over to you this victim, O Proserpina, or Acherusia [referring to the Underworld river of Acheron] if you prefer that I call you so. Summon for me the triple-headed hound [Cerberus] to snatch away the heart of Plotius. Promise that you will give him three gifts – dates, figs and a black pig – if he completes this before the month of March. These I will offer you, Proserpina Salvia, when you complete this in an orderly fashion.

I give over to you the head of Plotius, the slave of Avonia. Proserpina Salvia, I give over to you the head of Plotius. Proserpina Salvia, I give over to you the forehead of Plotius. Proserpina Salvia, I give over to you the eyebrows of Plotius Proserpina Salvia, I give over to you the eyelids of Plotius Proserpina Salvia, I give over to you the pupils of Plotius. Proserpina Salvia, I give over to you

— the nostrils, lips, ears, nose, tongue and teeth of Plotius, so that he may not be able to say what is causing him pain;

— the neck, shoulders, arms and fingers, so that he may not be able to aid himself in any way;

— his breast, liver, heart and lungs, so that he may not be able to discover the source of his pain;

— his intestines, stomach, navel and sides, so that he may not be able to sleep;

— his shoulder blades, so that he may not be able to sleep soundly;

— his 'sacred organ' so that he may not be able to urinate;

— his rump, anus, thighs, knees, shanks, shins, feet, ankles, heels, toes and toenails, so that he may not be able to stand by his own strength.

No matter what he may have written, great or small, just as he has written a proper spell and commissioned it [against me], so I hand over and consign Plotius to you, so that you may take care of him by the month of February. Let him perish miserably. Let him leave life miserably. Let him be destroyed miserably. Take care of him so that he may not see another month.

— John G. Gager, *Curse Tablets and Binding Spells from the Ancient World* (Oxford University Press, 1992)

It seems likely that Proserpina and Pluto would have got the general gist.

DRAMATIS PERSONAE

H ere is a list of some of the main players in the book, with age and death date (where known or hypothesized by ancient sources).

* − did not die naturally.
The average age is 66; the mean age is 63/64.

Aristotle 62, 322 BC: Greek biologist, philosopher, critic

Augustus (Octavian) 76, AD 14: heir of Julius Caesar, first Roman emperor

Aulus Cornelius Celsus *c.* 75, *c.* AD 50: Roman doctor

Cato the Elder 85, 149 BC: soldier and statesman

Cato the Younger* 49, 46 BC: great-grandson of the above, soldier and statesman

Cicero* 63, 43 BC: statesman, philosopher, orator and letter-writer

Galen *c.* 71, *c.* AD 201: famous Greek physician

Hippocrates *c.* 83, *c.* 377 BC: famous Greek physician

Homer, seventh century BC: Greek epic poet, author of the *Iliad* and the *Odyssey*

Horace 56, 8 BC: lyric poet

Julius Caesar* 56, 44 BC: soldier, statesman, dictator

Juvenal, *c.* AD 130: satirical poet

Lucretius ?45, *c.* 55 BC: atomist poet, wrote *On the Nature of the Universe*

Martial *c.* 62, *c.* AD 102: satirical poet

Petronius* AD 66: satirist in the court of Nero

Plato ?78, 347 BC: philosopher, disciple of Socrates

Pliny the Elder* 56, AD 79: wrote 37-book encyclopedia of the natural world

Pliny the Younger ?51, *c.* AD 112: senator, letter-writer

Plutarch ?75, after AD 120: Greek philosopher and biographer

Seneca the Younger* 64, AD 65: philosopher, adviser to Nero

Socrates* ?70, 399 BC: philosopher

Tacitus ?64, *c.* AD 120: historian of the early empire

Virgil 51, 19 BC: poet of the *Aeneid*

BIBLIOGRAPHY

Allason-Jones, L., *Women in Roman Britain* (British Museum Publications, 1989)

Attalus.org

Latin Inscriptions: Epitaphs: http://attalus.org/docs/cil/epitaph.html

Latin Inscriptions: Elogia: http://attalus.org/docs/cil/elogia.html#add.1

Barney, S. A., Lewis, W. J., Beach, J. A. and Berghof, O. (tr.), *The Etymologies of Isidore of Seville* (Cambridge University Press, 2006)

Bond, S., *Trade and Taboo: Disreputable Professions in the Roman Mediterranean* (University of Michigan Press, 2016)

Bradley, K. R., *Discovering the Roman Family. Studies in Roman Social History* (Oxford University Press, 1991)

Braund, S. M. and Gill, C. (eds.), *The Passions in Roman Thought and Literature* (Cambridge University Press, 1997)

Brickhouse, T. C. and Smith, N. D., *The Trial and Execution of Socrates* (Oxford University Press, 2001)

Carroll, M., *Spirits of the Dead: Roman Funerary Commemorations in Western Europe* (Oxford University Press, 2006)

Cokayne, K., *Experiencing Old Age in Rome* (Routledge, 2003)

Dover, K. J., *Greek Popular Morality in the Time of Plato and Aristotle* (Blackwell, 1974)

Edwards, C., *Death in Ancient Rome* (Yale University Press, 2007)

Eyben, E., *Restless Youth in Ancient Rome* (Routledge, 1993)

Falkner, T. M. and de Luce, J. (eds.), *Old Age in Greek and Latin Literature* (State University of New York, 1989)

Flower, H. I. (ed.), *The Cambridge Companion to the Roman Republic* (Cambridge University Press, 2004)

Green, R. M. (tr.), *Galen's* Hygiene (Illinois, 1951)

Harlow, M. and Laurence, R., *Growing Up and Growing Old in Ancient Rome* (Routledge, 2002)

Hope, V. M., *Roman Death: The Dying and the Dead in Ancient Rome* (Continuum, 2009)

Hope, V. M. and Huskinson, J. (eds.), *Memory and Mourning: Studies on Roman Death* (Oxbow, 2011)

Hopkins, K., *Death and Renewal* (Cambridge University Press, 1983)

Jones, P., *Veni Vidi Vici* (Atlantic, 2013)

Jones, P., *Quid Pro Quo* (Atlantic, 2016)

Keppie, L., *The Making of the Roman Army* (Batsford, 1984)

Kertzer, D. I. and Saller, P. (eds.), *The Family in Italy: From Antiquity to the Present* (Yale University Press, 1991)

King, H. (ed.), *Health in Antiquity* (Routledge, 2005)

Laes, C. and Strubbe, J., *Youth in the Roman Empire: The Young and Restless Years?* (Cambridge University Press, 2014)

Lattimore, R. A., *Themes in Greek and Latin Epitaphs* (Illinois, 1942)

Lefkowitz, M. R. and Fant, M. B., *Women's Life in Greece and Rome* (Bloomsbury, 2016)

Leroi, A. M., *The Lagoon: How Aristotle Invented Science* (Bloomsbury, 2014)

McKeown, J. C., *A Cabinet of Ancient Medical Curiosities* (Oxford University Press, 2017)

Minois, G., *History of Old Age: From Antiquity to the Renaissance* (University of Chicago Press, 1989)

Morgan, T., *Popular Morality in the Early Roman Empire* (Oxford University Press, 2007)

Parker, H. N. (tr.), *Censorinus: The Birthday Book* (University of Chicago Press, 2007)

Parkin, T., *Old Age in the Roman World* (The Johns Hopkins University Press, 2003)

Parkin, T. and Pomeroy, A. J., *Roman Social History: A Sourcebook* (Routledge, 2007)

Payne, T., *The Ancient Art of Growing Old* (Vintage, 2015)

Rawson, B., *Children and Childhood in Roman Italy* (Oxford University Press, 2003)

Rawson, B. and Weaver, P. (eds.), *The Roman Family in Italy: Status, Sentiment, Space* (Oxford University Press, 1997)

Saller, R. P., *Patriarchy, Property and Death in the Roman Family* (Cambridge University Press, 1994)

Shelton, J., *As the Roman Did* (Oxford University Press, 1998)

Toner, J., *Roman Disasters* (Polity, 2013)

———, *The Ancient World* (Profile, 2015)

Verboven, K. and Laes, C. (eds.), *Work, Labour and Professions in the Roman World* (Brill, 2016)

Versnel, H. S., *Coping with the Gods: Wayward Reading in Greek Theology* (Brill, 2011)

Walker, H. J. (tr.), *Valerius Maximus: Venerable Deeds and Sayings* (Hackett, 2004)

Those translations that are not acknowledged are either my own or derive (with occasional modifications) from the various online, mainly Loeb-based, sites.

INDEX

A NOTE ABOUT
THE AUTHOR

Peter Jones was educated at Cambridge University and taught Classics at Cambridge and at Newcastle University, before retiring in 1997. He has written a regular column, 'Ancient & Modern', in the *Spectator* for many years and is the author of various books on the Classics, including the bestselling *Learn Latin* and *Learn Ancient Greek*, as well as *Reading Virgil: Aeneid I and II, Vote for Caesar, Veni, Vidi, Vici, Eureka!* and *Quid Pro Quo*.